Being Human
A User Guide
Why we do what we do

Anne Burton

Copyright © 2018 Anne Burton

All rights reserved.

This book is sold subject to the conditions that it shall not, by way of trade or otherwise, be lent hired out, or otherwise circulated without the author's prior consent in any form of binding or cover other than that in which it is published or without a similar condition, including this condition, being imposed on the subsequent purchaser.

ISBN:1533606811
ISBN-13:9781533606815

www.being-human.today

DEDICATION

To Roy and Rachel, who have survived my improvisational parenting skills with style and a great sense of humour

If, at this point, you are hoping that I had an epiphany and realised the one thing, the blinding flash of inspiration, that was going to fix this mess for me and that I am going to share this pearl of wisdom with you now, I'm afraid you are going to be disappointed. I don't know who these (rather annoying) people are who realise that they need to change and just go right ahead and change, but I am clearly not one of them, as the first thing I did was to go straight back in and try to carry on doing exactly what I had been doing. Only more so. And what do you do when you are already at a breaking point and stressed out of your mind? You get on with it and sign up to do an MBA, of course, because that'll show them!

The final year of the MBA programme took place at the worst and best of timing. I was in terrible shape, but what I learnt during that year about behaviour and why we do what we do formed the basis of my new-found passion. I read and went on courses learning everything I could about how we decide who we are and why we do what we do. It was illuminating, and I could see how patterns of behaviour had formed and beliefs had become so deeply embedded that I had mistaken them for absolute truth. I was fascinated but also came to realise that, while I now was aware of my beliefs and behaviours, that was exactly what I had – awareness, but nothing I could do about any of it. And so, the search continued. More books and more courses. This time, it was about change techniques, mindset, hypnosis – anything that could help me move from where I was to where I wanted to be.

Through my study, I identified themes of behaviour and change; often, the terminology was different, but the underlying principle or outcome was remarkably similar. 'Same Horse Different Jockey' as a friend of mine would say. It became increasingly clear that whatever it was that you wanted to achieve or to change, there were aspects of being human that needed to be in balance and that the western world had somewhat neglected those aspects. Our focus on all things technical and our relentless drive to get more from less and to achieve success through material gain, meant that we did not focus on some of the aspects of being human that are not only desirable but essential if we are to lead a balanced life and retain our true humanity.

From birth, we are highly programmable beings. One of the reasons that human beings have been so successful at populating all but the most inhospitable places on the planet is our incredible adaptability. We are born with only about a third of our brains functioning as we need them to and develop the rest in response to our environment and the people we are with. Over our lives, we create and run programmes in our minds for doing everything from using cutlery to parenting the next generation. Some of these programmes run well, and some are less helpful, but we run them anyway, often oblivious to the fact that we are running them at all. We dip into some of the programmes when we need them – like an app: open it, do what you need to do and close it again. Others are more fundamental to how we function, our core programmes or operating system. If you don't have Windows or IOS set up right on your tablet or laptop, then your apps are not going to work well for you. The six programmes that make up our human operating system are very similar to this. Sometimes, they need a bit of attention, an upgrade or a reboot to support the day-to-day process of being human and to get us to where we want to be in our lives.

I am not telling you how you should live your life, what career you need to follow or how much exercise you should get. I'm not advising you to set yourself goals to achieve vast amounts of money or status or great sporting, business or artistic achievements because I don't know what you should do with your life or what you want to achieve – only you know that. This is about taking care of aspects of your life that will help you whatever it is that you decide to do – whether your aim is to climb all the mountains of the world or to keep chickens and grow organic broccoli, or both.

Consciousness, Communication, Connection, Courage, Creativity and Compassion… Paying attention to these six core programmes in our operating system will help us do whatever we choose to by making us more resilient, resourceful and balanced. The six programmes are all linked to and dependent upon eachother like cogs in a machine or atoms in a molecule; we need all of them for the system to function well. If we pay attention to any one of them, we can enhance the other aspects; if we exclude any one from our awareness, all the other aspects will feel the detrimental effect. They form a matrix more than a linear process, and you can choose to look at it from whatever perspective you find most useful. The following description deals with Consciousness, which also is the subject of the next chapter. I have chosen to deal with Consciousness first because one must start somewhere. To look at any of the other five, we need to bring them into our conscious thought processes, so it feels like a good place to begin.

Consciousness

> There are many differing opinions on what consciousness is and where it stems from. Some believe it is God given; some say it's just a by-product of chemicals in the brain and some that it is part of one vast universal consciousness. The bottom line is that we don't really know. All we do know is that we are having some sort of experience and that our consciousness is a part of that. It's how and what we think. How we make meaning,

create beliefs and decide who we are. How we select what we do and don't pay attention to and how we can use this to create change. It all starts with awareness.

Communication

As a species, we have developed increasingly sophisticated ways of communicating, and we are always communicating something to somebody. We do it so naturally that we take it for granted and assume our message has been received as we intended when it may have entirely missed the mark. But what is it that we are really communicating and what can we do to be in more conscious control of it?

Connection

We have a pack mentality, and the need for connection is fundamental to our survival, our experience as a human being and our very existence. There are parts of our brains that are hardwired to seek out and confirm our connection to others and our sense of belonging. So, what happens when we disconnect? What do we do when we feel like we don't belong? What do we do to fill the gap we create by disconnecting, and how can we get back the connection that we need?

Courage

Although we often think of courage in terms of acts of daring and bravado, courage is about being who we really are and resisting the seductive attraction of 'fitting in'. Creativity and innovation require the courage to put something new into the world knowing that it might not work. Change requires the courage to take yourself out into the world and take the risk that not everyone will love what you are doing.

Creativity

We are creative beings, but, frequently, we stifle this natural part of our make up because we aren't 'good' at art, or because our schools value science more. Somehow, we seem to have come to believe that science and creativity don't go together, and that we are either academic or creative – never both. Creativity is more than art. It's when we experiment, play and put anything new and unique out into the world – an idea, an invention or a solution to a problem.

Compassion

Compassion is arguably the most fundamental human emotion and may even have developed before our intelligence; yet, it is fragile and is often swept aside in the rush to do more, have more and be more. In our rush for success and to get on to the next rung on the promotion ladder, we tend to show little compassion to others, and often, none at all to ourselves. How did we become our own worse critics? Can't we be successful and compassionate at the same time?

Each of the following six chapters presents a combination of information and practical actions that you can take to refocus on each of the core programmes in your operating system. These are simple day-to-day practices that will help you maintain a balanced foundation to build on with whatever it is that you choose to do with your life.

It would be easy for me to tell you that simply reading the next six chapters will automatically rearrange your life in a way that makes you more resilient, more resourceful and more balanced in your response to things, and I would have liked to be able to say that it will. Sadly, it won't. This book is like the gym membership and the exercise bike you bought (yes, me too…). You will have to do something more than buying it and looking at it if you want to create any change.

Each chapter has a short section at the end entitled 'Something to Practice', where you will find some suggestions of things to look out for, listen for, say and do. These are not 'Life Hacks' tricks or quick fixes. They are just simple practices that can be easily adopted and developed by anyone in search of positive change. They can help in finding your balance in the way you operate and in providing a more solid foundation for whatever comes next.

There are some additional resources to help you along the way at www.being-human.today/resources.

2 CONSCIOUSNESS

'We don't need to eradicate the ego, we simply need to be conscious of the deeper self as well'- Tim Freke

It may seem strange to say that we need to focus on our consciousness when, other than the times when we sleep, we are conscious all the time. If you were not conscious, you would not be aware that you are reading this, would you? So, to talk about being conscious, we really need to talk about how unconscious we are and what that means for how we experience our lives.

Estimates vary, but the general consensus is that only up to about 5% of what goes on in our minds constitutes conscious thought – with everything else happening on autopilot in our unconscious processes. Think about it for a moment. Everything that we can do automatically, without having to think about it, is managed by our unconscious processes. Walking, running or reaching out an arm to pick something up are all things that we do automatically. You may have consciously decided to move, but do you know which muscle you need to move and in what order to move it to make your hand pick a cup? Once we have learned how to do it, we don't need to think about it anymore, and all this is done outside of our conscious awareness because to do it all consciously would be too much to deal with consciously all at the same time. A good example of this is driving. When you were learning to drive, you had to think consciously about every movement – looking in your mirrors, taking the handbrake off – everything needed your conscious attention. When you have been driving for a while, these things start to come naturally to you and you just get in and drive, without giving it much thought, to the point where your unconscious mind can take over the process. You suddenly find yourself five minutes down the road with no real memory of how you got there. It is like being in a light trance, and we live most of our lives in this state.

We have an incredibly complex brain that has evolved over time by adding on new thinking capabilities in new areas of the brain as our neurology developed. This is a bit like adding on an extension to a building; the old part is still there, but now you have some new space that is more up-to-date and can be used in ways for which the original building was not suited. So, what we have isn't so much one single large brain but more like three brains stacked on top of each other, working with differing levels of consciousness so that we can focus on specific tasks without having to consciously take care of everything that is going on in our mind and body.

To explain this a little more, just imagine, for a moment, that your brain is like a three-drawer filing cabinet with one of those little wire in-trays sitting on top of it.

In the Bottom Drawer

This is the oldest part of your brain where all those things that your mind does for you and that you never have to be conscious of are stored. Things like the way it keeps you alive while you are asleep, digests your food, sends out antibodies and white cells to heal and protect against infections. It regulates your breathing, your temperature, manages your hormones (or not!), heals wounds and generally does a pretty fantastic job of running your body and keeping you alive. The bottom drawer contains all your basic instincts; it lets your conscious mind know when you are hungry, too hot, too cold, or thirsty. It lets you know when there is a threat that you need to run away from or fight and when it's time to pass on your DNA to the next generation. Many thousands of years ago, this was all we needed; our existence was all about the survival of ourselves and our species, and that is what the bottom drawer takes care of.

The contents of the bottom drawer are already in place when we are born, and the processes run even before we make our appearance in the world. This is not to say that all this runs in isolation. The basic processes continue to run in the same way, but what causes them to run changes as we grow and learn. The two things that scare us instinctively are loud noises and a feeling of falling. If this remained the same, we wouldn't last very long when faced with, say, a large hungry carnivore, so we must learn what does and doesn't pose a threat to us. This is where the second or middle drawer of your brain's filing cabinet comes in.

When we have an experience, the information from that experience gets into our brain through our five senses of sight, sound, feeling, taste and smell for processing and action or filing for future reference.

There is a lot of information in an experience beyond what we can process and hold on to all at once; so, our brain focusses very quickly on what it thinks the important elements of the experience are. It does this very efficiently but, as you will see, not always very effectively. We will either delete some information from the experience as irrelevant, distort it to fit something we have experienced before or generalise it to group it together with other similar experiences and save processing time the next time we have a similar experience. Sound complicated? Here is an example:

A small child is in the park for the first time since he/she started to walk. A safe and trusted adult is holding his/her hand. It is a warm sunny day, and other children are playing and laughing close by. As they walk through the park, a dog, passing in the opposite direction with its owner, barks excitedly at a ball that has been thrown. None of the other children notice, and the child's parent is still holding his/her hand safely, but the child is startled and **Deletes** all the information that indicates that he/she is safe. He/she then focusses entirely on the loud noise coming from the dog and gets scared and cries. The child's parent is surprised by the sudden crying for what seems to be no apparent reason and quickly scoops the child up to find out what the problem is, inadvertently reinforcing the belief that there is a threat.

On another trip out a few days later, the child sees a similar dog. The middle filing cabinet produces the nearest similar experience focussed on the dog, to save processing time (because our brains are efficient like that), and the child is scared again as their brain **Distorts** the image of this dog to be the same as the last dog (i.e. loud and scary). So, now the child has two experiences where they have felt unsafe in the presence of a dog despite all evidence to the contrary, and the brain then **Generalises** these experiences into 'All dogs are scary' which saves a lot of processing time whenever a dog is close by.

This information gets stored in the middle drawer but can be passed very quickly to the bottom drawer. Whenever a dog is present, where a small almond-shaped part of the brain called the amygdala acts like a burglar alarm and sets of the fight or flight response, and the body gets ready to run or fight or hide.

You can see how this would have been a very useful and life-extending skill to have when the threats we were facing were very real threats to our existence. Being able to respond quickly without having to stop and think could make the difference between having dinner and being dinner, but our brains do this with all of our experiences. They get filed in the middle drawer where they form our blueprint of what the world is like and who we are in that world. Even if, for example, the experience was about how to use a chair or that it's a good idea to look both ways before you cross the road. It would either be a waste of brain space or even dangerous to have to figure either of these out every time we had a similar experience – a different chair or a different road – but our brain does not hang about to see if the pattern is rational or helpful; it only cares that there is a pattern and will go with the closest similar experience in the filing cabinet every time. This is why we get ready to run or fight when faced with the perceived threat of an overdue bill, getting cut up on a roundabout or a meeting with the boss.

All our experiences are interpreted, compared and stored in this way. We scan the filing cabinet to see if there is anything similar to our current experience in there and then use that to guide our response and behaviour to this event.

This is where stress can start to become a problem for us. The bottom drawer processes responds to some information from the middle drawer that says there is a threat present and sets off the alarm. Adrenaline and cortisol flood through our body in preparation for running or fighting, which, if we do run or fight, will be naturally used up in the process. When the threat is an unpayable bill or yet another red light that is going to make us late, there is no fight to have and nowhere to run; so, all the chemicals that have been released in preparation for that have no job to do and can have a detrimental impact on our health and well-being. Becoming more aware of what meaning we make of things and consciously recreate that meaning can go a long way towards taking some of the unnecessary and unhelpful stress out of our lives.

In the Middle Drawer

As we developed, our way of life became more complex – growing away from one of pure survival and into one of co-operative groups or tribes sharing responsibilities and creating safety in the numbers of the group where different things became important.

It became as important to fit in with and be accepted by the tribe as to scan the horizon for danger because to be rejected or cast out by the tribe could be just as life-threatening. Using the same processes of Distorting, Deleting and Generalising the information from our experiences and comparing it against what we already have in the filing cabinet, we identified not just physical threats but also what we had to do to be acceptable to the group, what our place was, where the limits to the acceptability were and what we must do to avoid rejection. We continue to filter and interpret the information from our experiences in the same way to this day and then store that interpretation along with all of the others. This becomes our beliefs about everything from the correct use of cutlery to whether we feel like we fit in at work, or our body image, whether we think we can't trust others or even ourselves. Our beliefs then form the basis of our values – what is important to us, what is and is not acceptable and how we decide what is right and wrong.

Beliefs can form either because of a significant individual event or a string of similar events. An experience that is highly emotional can create a belief without us being conscious of what we have decided, and it doesn't mean we can't change that decision.

Changing the way our programmes run can happen in the same way, either a one-off event or revelation that changes our mind and belief from that point on or by deliberate repetition over a period of time. Changing is just another form of learning; sometimes, we pick things up straight away, and for some projects, we have to practice.

Along with the skills of filtering and making meaning, the unconscious part of our mind also likes to be right and has a very clever way of consistently proving that it is.

We have something called a Reticular Activating System, which is, thankfully, shortened to RAS. It is, in effect, the Google search bar of your brain. Whatever you put in there, your brain will go off and seek out examples to bring to your attention. For example, when you decide to buy a new car, have you noticed how you suddenly start seeing the very make, model and colour that you are interested in everywhere you go? They were, of course, always there. It's just that your brain had deleted them as unimportant until you put them in the search bar. This very clever search facility is a great invention if you are scanning the horizon for hungry predators or something that might become today's dinner. Not so helpful though where some of our less empowering beliefs are concerned, because if you are telling yourself that you are not good enough in some way, or that things just don't work out for you and other people are cleverer, happier, more talented etc., guess what your search bar will look for? No prizes for this one. It will look for evidence that what you believe is true and delete or distort evidence to the contrary. You might have heard people saying 'That always happens to me' or 'Things never go the way I want them to', which are two huge generalisations and just the type of thing people say when they are confirming to themselves that their beliefs, however unhelpful, are correct.

I am not saying that all you need to do is believe something and it will be true; you might need to take some action too. I don't believe I can play the piano because, currently, I can't, but I believe I could if I took lessons and practiced. So, a belief change is a first step rather than a magical wand, but if you believe you can't do something, then you won't. Even if you set off every now and again to try to do it, the belief will at some point stop you, if only to find more evidence for you that your belief is correct.

The Top Drawer

So, the bottom drawer of the filing cabinet is highly adept at all things that relate to our physical survival and maintenance of our body, and the middle drawer is a more emotional place looking for relationships between events and people and how we get accepted by and stay with our tribe. The top drawer is for complex problem solving and is where all our creative thinking, rationalisation and logical reasoning gets done.

The first thing to point out about the top and newest part of the filing cabinet is that, while it is very good at problem-solving, it is also, in comparison with the other two drawers, very slow, and so a pattern from the middle drawer or a fight and flight response from the bottom drawer can have us reacting to a situation before the top drawer can weigh up what's going on and generate a better course of action. The top drawer is great in unemotional, non-threatening situations where it can gather information, test scenarios and come up with a great solution to whatever project you have set for it. As soon as you are in a situation that, according to the records in the middle drawer, could be a problem for you, everything changes and the fast response safety settings of the middle and lower drawers kick in.

For example, imagine that you have a presentation to do at work. You are very familiar with the subject and prepare a great presentation that you can do without notes because you know the content inside out… Until you get in the room! The moment you stand up to speak, your mouth goes dry. You start to trip over your words, you can feel your palms sweat. The more you notice this, the worse it gets and you 'Umm' and 'err' your way through the presentation, miss out key points and lose the flow of what you had so carefully prepared. When you get outside after completing it, you could kick yourself because you know this stuff!! The speed of response when we perceive a threat (real or imagined) is faster than our ability to generate a rational, considered response.

This said, the top drawer of the cabinet is incredibly clever and is responsible for so many great achievements and inventions that it's impossible to list them. Just think about any piece of technology, construction, medical breakthrough, and you will have an example of what the top drawer is capable of.

It's no real surprise then that we have highly valued the thinking of the brain's top drawer for many years – often almost neglecting our other thought processes. We have prioritised rational thinking conscious mind in the western world to the point of dismissing what goes on in the bottom and middle drawers. We have attempted to separate the rational and the logical as if we believe that we can separate that part of our mind from the rest and always have our intellect in charge regardless of what happens and what our middle and bottom drawers tell us.

It's a recipe for disaster in the long run and something of which we are at last becoming aware, with mindfulness and meditation being on the increase, as we try to redress the balance between the slow but rational and the quick and intuitive.

This is not about turning the tables and valuing intuition and belief over rational and logical thinking because here's the thing; we learn a lot from our top drawer. New concepts, ideas and skills are all picked up first through our conscious thinking and then made rational in the newest part of our brains before becoming something we know or can do unconsciously. So, working with and focussing on consciousness needs all three drawers to be in on the act so that we can bring things like unhelpful beliefs, into our conscious awareness, learn something new from them and return a new belief to the middle drawer for future reference.

The in-tray

And finally, we get all the way up to the in-tray sitting on the top of the filing cabinet. This is where you hold anything that you are currently conscious of. The problem is that this is quite a shallow basket that can only hold between five and nine things at the same time, averaging at seven, and so, sometimes, things spill over when the tray gets too full.

When you leave the house in the morning, you realise that you need to get some fuel for the car but you are also thinking about what you are going to say in this morning's meeting, that you need to get something for dinner, that you have a dentist appointment, that the gas bill is overdue, and you must pay that online, that your knee is hurting when you press the brake and you think maybe it might be time to change your contact lenses' prescription and...and you have just driven past the petrol station.

Thoughts pop up from our middle drawer into our in-tray all the time. The more we pay attention to one kind of thought, the more our mind will find us similar thoughts to focus on, and although information flows between all the drawers in the filing cabinet and the in-tray all the time, it doesn't always flow freely. Our love for patterns, logic and top-drawer thinking puts up a barrier between what we believe we already know and thoughts or experiences that don't fit with our model of the world. Critical thinking and over rationalising often get in the way of new possibilities and being open to the idea that there is more to our experience than we know. We quickly compare every experience against what we already believe and deny or discard things that don't fit well with what is already held on file.

One of the times when we let this critical guard down is when we watch a film or read a story, when we suspend our disbelief and let imagination overrule logic, allowing us to accept the possibility of what we see on the screen. We don't sit there thinking 'How ridiculous! A man can't fly!' We just enjoy watching Superman. Allowing our critical thinking to relax a little helps us to get in touch, not only with imagination but also with some of the beliefs and processes we are running in the middle drawer, and the more self-talk happens in our heads, the harder it can be to bypass this critical thinking process.

Because the in-tray is so small, what we put in there is important, just as how often we do and how long we keep it there for, which is sometimes more important. Your RAS is scanning the in-tray as well as the first and second drawer. The items that are in the in-tray are what we are consciously focussed on, and our brain's search engine will very obediently go out and find evidence to support it, which means it can become cluttered with thoughts that are not necessarily helpful and block us from focussing on more resourceful ways of thinking. The more clutter we keep in the in-tray, the less conscious we become. When we keep a list of doubts, regrets and worries playing on a loop, there is no space for new information, new experience or just space for the sake of having some space.

How much of our potential experience do we miss because we are still re-running last night's argument, tomorrow's meeting or the to-do list on repeat? Our experience is in the present moment, but we focus most of our thinking on what happened in the past and what may or may not happen in the future. There is nothing wrong with reviewing how an event has gone or planning for the future, but when we do this all the time, we can become overwhelmed with regrets about the past and anxiety about the future because we don't tap into our resourcefulness by focussing on the Now.

The importance of learning to focus consciously on one thing at a time has thankfully begun to come back into our awareness as the myth of multitasking fades because unless the things we are doing are ones that we can do unconsciously, we cannot multi-task. When a task requires our conscious attention, we can only really do one thing at one given moment, and multi-tasking is just paying very brief moments of attention to different tasks sequentially, so each task gets the briefest of attention before the next one takes a moment of our time. It gives the appearance of doing many things all at the same time when it is just divided attention. It doesn't lead to satisfying or even necessarily acceptable results and is often a contributing factor to stress and anxiety levels that are difficult to manage. Mindfulness and meditation become increasingly becoming mainstream activities, even in the business world, which is traditionally the place where logic, rationalising and multitasking take pride of place. It is worth working on if you don't already, and just clocking up eleven hours of cumulative meditation (not all at once, as you will be pleased to hear) will change how your brain works for the better. We form new neural connections, and our resilience and resourcefulness increase as we can more easily pull our attention back from the past or the future to consider the action we can take in the present. Keep pursuing whatever meditation or mindfulness practice suits you best. It doesn't have to be about sitting still. There are many forms of moving meditation, including walking, Tai Chi, and Qi Gong or Yoga – whatever suits you best. The important thing is to de-clutter the in-tray and enhance your ability to focus on one thing at a time.

I am not a natural meditator, but I know it's a good and healthy practice to get into, and so I persist, despite (or possibly because of) my very noisy, chatty mind. Some of my early attempts went something like this in my head:

'OK, twenty minutes meditation, no problem.... Deep breath.... Relax.... Concentrate on your breathing.... In.... Out.... My nose itches.... Ignore your nose, concentrate on your breathing.... OK.... In.... Out.... Did I switch the cooker off? No! Focus on your breathing! OK, OK.... Breathing. OK. That chicken is a bit small, will it feed all of us? What are you thinking about chickens for? You are supposed to be meditating.... Oh, sod it, I'm not good at this!'

It went on like this for some time. It's no surprise that getting frustrated about not being able to do it did nothing to improve my technique or my results until a friend gave me a useful suggestion. Whenever I noticed that I had wandered off to think about chickens or itchy noses or whatever tangent I had gone off on, I just had to say to myself: *Just thinking*' and refocus on the meditation. Over time, this has helped to extend the time I can focus without too much interruption from the clutter in my in-tray.

What are you cluttering up your in-tray with? What unhelpful beliefs and stress-inducing lists of things you need to do but haven't are taking up the space needed to take you forward?

Something to Practice - Being Mindful and Mindless

Being Mindful – What's in the In-Tray? It all starts with awareness. So, that's where we are going to start with here. There are two aspects to what we are going to look at in the in-tray. Clutter and Nonsense.

Clutter – We use up a lot of the spaces in our in-tray with stuff that just doesn't need to be there, and it gets in the way of being able to focus on what does matter.

Before you leave work, write down what you have to do the day after and leave it there on the desk.

Before you go to bed, or start to meditate, write down what you have to do or what is occupying your mind and leave it downstairs or anywhere out of sight.

When you notice thoughts like 'I must remember to…' or 'Oh, I still haven't…', write them down in a diary or the calendar on your phone.

Take out your task list from your head and put it on paper; it frees up space and helps stop the treadmill of reciting lists in your head. This can significantly contribute to how stressed or overwhelmed you feel. Be aware though that you may forget to do this when you first start, which is why this section is called 'Something to Practice' and not 'Something to be instantly good at'. Just start again, and it will become a part of how you do what you do.

Nonsense – The nonsense in the in-tray is all the thoughts that start with *'I can't ever…', 'It never...', 'It always…'* and *'They always...'* You know the stuff I'm talking about. Those thoughts that your search engine has looked for evidence of until you believe them and stop taking action towards what you really want in life. This practice is about choosing and changing what you put in your mind's search engine.

When you catch yourself repeating thoughts like 'never', 'always', 'won't' and 'can't', find and notice examples that contradict that belief.

If, for example, you often find yourself thinking that things are not working out for you, start to notice these examples – however small they may be. Start with really simple things. Notice and write down everything that has gone according to plan with everyday plans and activities. The more you practice it, the more your search engine will search for that evidence until it becomes a habit and your mind just starts doing it for you.

Being Mindless – The creative power of the mindless task

Allowing your mind to wander while doing a simple repetitive task has two main benefits. First, if you are actively worrying about something, by giving your body something to do and taking some of the focus away from whatever problem is sitting in your in-tray, you can lower your stress levels. Second, while your mind is distracted by the activity you are engaged in, your unconscious mind can go to work unhindered by the constant chatter coming from the in-tray and find some creative alternative and solutions for you to consider.

When you find yourself wrestling with a problem and stuck without a way forward or a solution, find a simple, repetitive but active task to do and focus as much as you can on the process of doing that task. When I say focus, I don't mean replace the chatter in your head about the problem with chatter in your head about the task you are doing; that is just not helpful. What I mean is, focus on engaging all your senses in noticing the task, and just let your mind wander. If it wanders back to the problem, bring your awareness back to the task.

IMPORTANT – When your mind wanders back to the problem, don't give yourself grief about it.

Instead, say to yourself; *'Just thinking'* and go back to focussing on the task.

And what can the task be? Pretty much anything you can do mindlessly. Clean the windows, walk your dog (or borrow one) or get a colouring book (seriously, the mandala ones are great for this). I even know someone who finds that ironing is good for this (I'm planning to send him mine to do!).

3 COMMUNICATION

The single biggest problem in communication is the illusion that it has taken place. - George Bernard Shaw

As a species, our skill with communication, and the many ways we have developed to do more of it to larger audiences more of the time, is staggering. On top of our daily face-to-face interactions, there are so many other ways that other human beings communicate with us – television, social media, radio, music, advertising, branding – the list is long and the amount of information hitting our senses every day is almost unimaginable.

With the growth of the internet and satellite communication, our daily exposure to information is now roughly five times what it was 30 years ago. This is a big enough increase in itself, but when you stop to think about it, we are probably exposed to more information in a couple of days than we would have been exposed to in a lifetime only a few hundred years ago. Only as far back as the early seventeenth century, many people couldn't read or write; there were no electronic means of communicating, and newspapers didn't exist. Communication was reliant on face-to-face conversations or handwritten documents, for those who could read, and a far cry from the world of the internet and instant information that we are familiar with today.

The human mind, however, has not significantly expanded its capacity to process and interpret information. Our capacity to absorb information is still what it was in simpler, less data cluttered times. Recent research does suggest that we are becoming more intelligent, but we are still working with the same equipment; it has not grown in processing power at the same rate as the data available for processing has. We still use the Distort, Delete and Generalise methods to make sense of the world that we looked at in the last chapter, working with our personal interpretation of events based on what we already have in the filing cabinet, which is far from perfect information.

It is no real surprise then that we can so frequently have instances of misunderstanding and miscommunication in our lives. Whether it's at work or at home, we spend a lot of time and energy clearing up the aftermath of communication that has gone wrong. Just to demonstrate the size of the issue, in 2014, a study estimated that misunderstanding written agreements cost every adult in the UK an average of £428 or a total of £21 billion per year. This is just one aspect of communication, and it only looks at a financial effect. Now, consider how much time we waste, how much frustration is caused and how many relationships are damaged beyond repair by not being conscious of what we are communicating. Then, you can start to get a feel for the importance of this to our life experience.

So, the question is, when we are swimming in a sea of data, how can we be sure of what we are communicating to whom? More importantly, maybe, what are other people trying to tell us that we are missing because our data processing system is already full?

There are two important things to be aware of with communication. First, you are doing it all the time. You cannot, in fact, not communicate. Even when you aren't speaking, your lack of words will be communicating something. The way you sit, walk or dress, your tone and speed of speech, your accent or dialect, the car you drive, the books you read, even if you are not present, your absence has a message in it. Second, the message is often not interpreted as we intend it to be. Other people can and do very easily take a different meaning from our communication than we intended, and we can do the same too, which is something we need to be very conscious of in our conversations.

Consider this for a moment if you will: 'The meaning of the communication is the response that you get.' This means that if you don't get the response that you are looking for, change the way you communicate.

We can, of course, just shrug and say: 'That's not what I meant, they have just taken it the wrong way'. This will not help us to be understood, and it's also a rather arrogant assumption. It assumes that what goes on in our head is the correct perception of the world and anything that doesn't align to that is incorrect – dangerous territory to be in and a position that is fertile ground for separation, prejudice and conflict to grow.

Once we accept the possibility of everything being an interpretation or a different perspective, then we can change the conversation when our attempt to communicate doesn't go the way we had hoped. I'm not saying that we can always get to a perfect mutual understanding, but when we take responsibility for our communication, we can get a lot closer to that possibility.

The other thing here is that we are also responsible for how we react to communication we receive from other people. It might seem a little unfair or unbalanced that we are responsible for how someone reacts to what we say and are also responsible for how we react. It seems like we are taking all of the responsibility here, and we are. Here is why:

You are the only person whose thoughts and actions you can directly access, and you are the only person that you can truly create change with. It is true that taking all the responsibility for your communication is not necessarily a popular position to take; there are many who would rather blame others for upsetting them and also blame them for being upset and *'taking it the wrong way'*. It is a convenient way to think that helps you avoid taking responsibility for anything. What I can tell you though is that the more you put responsibility for communication (or anything else in our lives) outside of yourself and in someone else's hands, the more powerless and dissatisfied you will feel. Taking responsibility doesn't mean we are taking the blame in some way. Responsibility means exactly what it sounds like; our ability to respond. So, this is about focussing on our Response-ability

What we say when we don't speak

Only about 7% of what we communicate in an emotional situation is the words that we use. The words are still important, and a massive 93% of our communication is our body language, tone, volume gesture and appearance.

How many times have you heard someone say, 'It wasn't what they said, it was the way they said it' or 'I could tell by the look on their face'? How often have you concluded that someone is not trustworthy or even dangerous because of how they move and/or what they wear?

One of the problems for us is that the big filing cabinet that is our unconscious mind tends to take everything personally. As far as it is concerned, your survival is what it is there to ensure; you are the centre of the universe, and therefore, everything that happens is about you. When we see an angry expression, hear a sharp tone of voice or contact someone who doesn't respond in a positive manner, our default position is not to think, 'I wonder what they are so upset about' or 'Perhaps, emailing them isn't the best way to get in touch with them.' Our default is to go to 'What are you getting angry with me for?' and 'They are ignoring me!' So, when you come in from work and bring the day's stress with you or arrive to meet friends without letting go of the hassle of getting ready around two kids who seem intent on killing each other, you can easily carry that body language and tone along with you. If you don't consciously adjust how you are carrying yourself, your expression and general demeanour from a tough day at the office can easily lead to an evening of bad-tempered exchanges at home as your family might think that your mood is about them and not about the day you have had.

Many people find it helpful to take a second or two to reset when moving between environments or events. They take a moment to be conscious of how they are moving, what tone they are using and what experience they want to create in the next interaction they have. It doesn't need to take long, and you can do it anywhere – in the carpark before you get out of the car, on the bus, in a corridor between meetings. Just taking a moment to de-clutter your in-tray and reset your body language can make a positive impact on your next conversation. It is not just other people who are affected by your body language.

If you are in any doubt about the connection between thoughts and their impact on the body, or the *mind-body connection*, consider for a moment the language that we use around emotional responses. We don't think nervous we feel nervous, and the same with stress, motivation, or any other emotion. We feel it in our body although it is our thoughts that initiate this response. We think about an event that we are concerned about and the chemical response that we trigger in doing this affects our digestion, heart rate and the amount that we sweat. Do this for long enough or often enough and we can start to experience more long-term effects like panic attacks, palpitations or IBS, as what we think about directly affects what goes on in our body.

This is not a one-way street. Just like what we do with our minds affects our body, what we do with our body can also have a profound effect on our state of mind. How we stand and move also works like a feedback loop, reminding us how we feel, impacting our behaviour and even our body chemistry. Similar to how our RAS will help our mind go out and find evidence that what we believe is true, the way we stand and move not only reflects how we are feeling but will actually create and reinforce that feeling.

When we feel confident we tend to stand and move confidently – we take up space in our environment and make larger, wider gestures when we speak. We hold our chin up and speak clearly. Taking up space like this is a demonstration of feeling powerful, and it's not just humans who do it. Take a look at any animal moving with confidence and they will all have similar traits – standing tall and straight and expanding their rib cages. It is a natural thing that we do to communicate our confidence.

When we do this, it lowers the level of our cortisol, also known as the stress hormone, and increases testosterone. Therefore, standing confidently increases confidence.

The opposite is also true. When we feel powerless, lacking confidence, stressed or depressed we stand and move as if we are collapsing in on ourselves. Our chin drops closer to our chest, our shoulders are hunched and rounded, we gesture infrequently and with small movements and our voice can be muted and lower in tone. It's almost as if we are keeping ourselves small and as low to the ground as we can. This is, again, a behaviour that you can see in many animals. Dogs slink low to the ground when they are submissive, apes and other primates will make themselves small when they feel powerless; this way of moving has the reverse effect on our body chemistry. Our testosterone levels will drop, and our cortisol levels will rise, and we will eventually strengthen this feeling of powerlessness. The way we work and use technology today does not help this situation, as using laptops, tablets and smartphones often means we are sitting in a hunched position with our chin down and making small, if any, movements. This increases the likelihood of feeling stressed and restricts our natural resourcefulness. This is another good reason to take a moment to reset. Consciously shifting to a more confident posture can boost your resourcefulness and productivity.

Be conscious of how you stand, your appearance and your tone. We can become so easily engrossed in the clutter and nonsense in our in-tray that we lose conscious connection with what we are communicating to ourselves and everyone around us. This behaviour is so common that 'Resting Bitch

Face' (a facial expression which unintentionally appears as if a person is angry, annoyed, irritated or contemptuous) is now a widely used phrase that even has an entry in the Urban Dictionary. So, clear the in-tray and be conscious of what your body is communicating to you and everyone else.

What we say when we do speak

If non-verbal communication wasn't complicated enough, things start getting really interesting when you throw words into the mix.

There are a couple of things that we are often not good at doing when we are having a conversation that are fundamental to communication actually taking place. One is listening, and the other is thinking about what we are saying. Given the way we go about communicating, that we ever come to any sort of consensus is borderline miraculous.

We don't listen when someone else is speaking to us – we don't truly listen in a way that would aid a deeper understanding of another person's experience. What we tend to do is run a search in our mind for the nearest similar thing to what is being talked about so that we can talk about our own experience as soon as the other person stops. Finding common ground or similar interests can help to build rapport, but the problem lies in us not stopping this behaviour after a relationship has been established. Add to this the complication that the person we are not really listening to is also not really thinking about how clear they are being in their choice of words. It is no surprise that often we can have a conversation or be in a meeting and think we are aligned only to find out that there are as many versions of the truth as there are people in the conversation.

The way that we process, group and label information means that the language we use when we are talking can be very ambiguous. The further we move from describing an object and towards ideas and concepts, the more ambiguous our language gets. If, for example, I asked you to pass me a banana, you would be pretty clear on what I meant by banana, and your interpretation of that word is likely to be very close to or the same as mine. If, on the other hand, I said that I wanted you to manage a situation for me, I know what I mean by 'manage', and you would know what you understand 'manage' to mean; and yet they could be very different.

Any word or phrase that could mean more than one thing sends our minds off in a search for what it means to us. Though each of us can have a different concept of what love is or what family means, we can still have a conversation about it as if we are talking about the same thing. It is easy to agree that love is important and never agree on what 'love' or 'important' really means to us.

Politicians and marketing companies make good use of the way we deal with ambiguous language:

Take Nike's 'Just Do It' campaign for example. Just what it is we should just do is not named, but we will make that connection ourselves. SKY's 'Believe in Better'. Better what? Better TV? Better Customer Service? Better cake? And better for who? Compared to what? All of these are left for us to join the dots. Barack Obama had millions of Americans saying 'Yes We Can' in agreement with each other and without knowing specifically who the 'we' referred to and what it was that they were agreeing they could do.

This is great for gaining group agreement and equally good at creating confusion. The antidote to this confusion is to be more specific. To check for understanding both in what we say and what we hear.

A very simple example of this is in something a friend told me about getting a little girl ready to go out. Her mum needed to fasten her coat and told her to turn around, so the little girl turned around a full 360 degrees instead of turning to face her mum, as her mum had meant but not said.

Some of us are big-picture thinkers and talk in concepts and generalisations; some of us are detail-thinkers and talk in specifics, and some of us move in between the two. Big-picture thinkers will agree very quickly about what they are going to do and then go off in different directions because no one had agreed specifically on how they were going to carry out their plan. Detail-thinkers will often take a long time to get started because they argue over the detail but not agree on an overall purpose or objective. The greater difficulty is when you get a big-picture person and a detail thinker attempting to communicate with each other approaching the subject from the opposite ends of the spectrum. The detail thinker will get frustrated because the big-picture person won't talk about the specifics, and the big-picture person will get frustrated because the detail thinker wants to talk about the minute details before the overall goal has been agreed upon.

To get a big-picture person to focus on the detail, you need to ask how, what, when and where questions to get into the specifics of the subject. For detail thinkers, you need to ask a question like 'What purpose or result or outcome are we looking for?' This will get them back up to the bigger picture or purpose of what they are doing. It is like climbing up and down a ladder between the ambiguous and the specific; it is not difficult once we are aware of how people prefer to think and talk.

Most of us talk in big-picture terms when we tell people what is going on in our lives and frequently generalise by saying 'People don't like…', 'Everybody thinks…', 'Nobody does that…' and so on. The who, what, where and when questions can recover the information that is missing from what we are saying to them. 'Which people?', 'Who is everybody?' and 'What?... Nobody?' will all help to get a deeper understanding of what a person is actually talking about. Be careful not to overdo the questioning; even though incomplete information can be frustrating, over questioning can be annoying, so pace yourself into the practice of doing this.

You may have noticed, though, that one questioning word that we like to use a lot is missing from the list of questions to ask to get more detail from big-picture people. The missing word is 'why'. The reason that it is missing is because asking 'why' often has the effect of putting the other person on the defensive. They are being asked to give a reason rather than being asked for more information, and it can carry with it an element of judgment. Asking 'Why did you do that?' can elicit a very different response than asking 'How did you decide to do that?' or 'What was your purpose in doing that?' This is not to say that you should never ask 'why'. Just be conscious of doing it and the effect it can have. Anyone who has spent time with small children can tell you how exhausting repeated 'why' questioning can be.

There are some words that we scatter throughout our day-to-day conversations to stay in the detailed for a while longer. They may be small and seemingly unimportant but can have a big impact on the meaning we take from the communication. Three of these words are 'and', 'but' and 'don't'.

When we put the word 'but' in a sentence, it deletes or minimises everything that was said before it (exchanging it for 'however' is not a solution as 'however' is just a slightly polished way of saying 'but' and has the same effect).

Have you ever been in a performance review and your manager tells you half a dozen things you have done well and then says 'but' before they tell you the thing you need to work on and all you can really focus on is that one thing that you didn't do well enough? That is the 'but effect'. If they had said 'and' instead, the impact would have been very different. In our minds, the only thing that is relevant is what comes after the 'but'.

As you may have realised already, using 'and' has the opposite effect and leaves all of the information intact. This doesn't mean that you shouldn't use 'but'. Just be conscious of when you are using 'and' and 'but' and the effect it can have on how your communication is received.

And finally, 'don't'.

The way we process language means that we don't focus directly on the word 'don't' but on the subject being talked about. So, if you are on a diet and you are thinking 'Don't buy any chocolate, don't buy any chocolate', the word that you RAS is picking up is 'chocolate'. You end up focussing on it rather than avoiding it.

We are very good at articulating what we don't want and need to practice more on saying specifically what it is that we do want. We say, 'Don't forget' rather than 'Remember'. We say, 'Don't run' rather than 'Walk'. We say, 'Don't make a mess' rather than 'Keep the place clean'.

Sometimes, we do need to tell people what we don't want, and we need to back that up straight away with what we do want; otherwise, how would they know?

This doesn't just apply to the word 'don't', it also applies to a lot of negatives in our language like 'mustn't' and 'shouldn't'. The important thing is to focus on what you do want so that your mind knows what to go in search of.

Something to Practice – Powerful Actions, Powerful Words

Stand Like a Superhero

When you feel that you need a confidence boost for a presentation or to handle a difficult situation or when you have been sitting hunched over your tablet, phone or computer for too long, spend a couple of minutes doing the following exercise. Repeat it as often as you like. The more you tell your body you feel confident and resourceful, the more it will become your everyday state.

Find a space where you won't be disturbed for a minute or two (lock yourself in the toilet if you need to!) and do one of the following for two minutes:

1) Stand with your feet shoulder-width apart. Put your hands on your hips, lift your chin so that you are looking upwards slightly without having to move your eyes. Broaden your rib cage and breathe smoothly and deeply (picture Superman or Wonder Woman, and you will have a good idea of what this pose looks like).
2) Sit on a chair (your car seat will do nicely for this) and lean back into the backrest so that your hips are slightly forward on the seat. With your feet on the floor, keep your knees wider apart than the width of your hip and your feet pointing away to the sides (in a 'ten to two' position). Clasp your hands behind your head so that your elbows are pointing away from you. Lift your chin up and breathe smoothly and deeply.

If you are doing this ahead of a specific event that you are not feeling confident about, it will also help to visualise yourself having successfully completed whatever it was that was worrying you as you stand or sit in your Superhero pose.

Get your 'but' out of the way

Practice those small, powerful words.

1) Practice consciously choosing whether to use 'and' or 'but'. Remember that 'but' deletes anything you say before it, so it is good for softening bad news, e.g. 'We lost the game on Saturday, BUT there are still 6 more games to come' sounds very different from 'We lost the game on Saturday, AND there are still 6 more games to come'. Likewise, if you are giving someone some feedback and want to focus on the good stuff as well as suggest areas for improvement, 'You did a very good piece of work, AND I'd like more information' will be better received than 'You did a very good piece of work, BUT I'd like more information'.

2) Practice saying what you do want instead of what you don't. If you do have to tell someone what you don't want them to do, back it up straight away with what you do want them to do. For example, replace 'Don't make a mess' with 'We need to keep that place tidy' or just 'Let's make sure we keep the place tidy'. The first step is to notice all the times that you talk about and focus on the things that you do not want and then to tag on the thing that you do want with the aim of replacing it altogether over time.

4 CONNECTION

'The opposite of addiction is not sobriety, it's human connection' -Johan Hari

It is easier, now more than ever, to contact another human being. We can fly to the other side of the world in a day; we can speak to and see people anywhere at any time; we can instantly send messages via different media, and yet, we are more disconnected from each other than ever.

We live in isolation; single person households are on the rise. We live next door to, opposite from, above and below people we don't know. Loneliness, which is also reported to be on the rise, increases the release of stress hormones and the likelihood of several life-threatening illnesses. Addiction to everything from class A drugs to gambling, shopping and working are rife as we struggle to fill the gap left by a lack of the most fundamental of human needs.

We need connection to other human beings more than anything else, which might sound dramatic but our feeling of connection and safety is the platform on which we build our identity, and we can't exist without an identity. This is, for us, quite literally a fate worse than death, and we seek a safe connection with another human being from the moment we are born. We are too small and dependent to make it on our own; we need someone to rely on, someone who can provide that security and attachment which, for humans, is needed for at least sixteen to twenty years, or longer, before we are ready to go at it alone.

Before we look at childhood experiences and what it can mean for us as adults, I want to make something really clear. The purpose of this is to bring a little clarity to how we grow up to have the beliefs we hold about ourselves and the world we live in. It is not in any way a criticism of us as parents or the parenting that we received. We are all doing the best we can with what is, at best, imperfect information. We raise our children based on our own experiences and beliefs and what our own parents taught us, and they did exactly the same – as did their parents and so on back to the dawn of time. We make adjustments as we go and do what we hope and believe is the best for our families. Sometimes we get it right and sometimes we don't. Sometimes the advice we get is good, and sometimes it isn't. We are just working with what we have.

First Connections

A new baby needs closeness, a skin-to-skin connection, at first, and a steadily developing tolerance to being further away, growing over the years until the baby grows into a fully independent adult. The success of this process can be seen in the way that we interact in adult relationships and in those with our own children. Most of us do have what could be called a 'good enough' attachment to those who care for us, and even then, the effect of early insecurities can be seen. People who are very clingy or 'needy' in relationships or people who avoid getting close to others or leap from one disastrous relationship to another disastrous relationship do so in part because of how the early attachment process was for them.

In theory, the process of attachment is straightforward; you keep your babies close and attend to them. Over time they will investigate their world more and more and rely less and less on you being close at hand. You see it happening over a much shorter timescale with animals; it is the natural way of things as offspring venture into the world and come back to base when they need reassurance that all is well. The problem for us is that the rules surrounding how we should look after our children combined with the demands of our changing lifestyles have made this process more difficult, and in some cases, all but dismissed its value entirely. It isn't simply a matter of ensuring that a child is fed and clean and warm, they can have all of these things and yet struggle to thrive. Many of us will have seen news images of children rocking by themselves in the overcrowded orphanages of war-torn countries. They don't rock from lack of food; they rock from lack of contact and interaction. Although this is an extreme example of the effects of lack of connection, it is just one end of the scale when we look at how vital human connection is to our development and well-being. Changes in advice and guidelines around the care of children has impacted our experience both of having and being a baby to a greater or lesser degree depending on where and when we were born.

Mothers have, in the past, been encouraged to let their children cry to 'exercise their lungs' as if breathing in and out is not exercise enough. Strict feeding regimes, allowing babies to 'cry it out' and resisting the urge to pick your baby up when he/she cries so as not to make them needy and clingy. These are just a few of the counter-intuitive rules that impact how safe a small child feels, and these, of course, don't even touch on the impact of any neglect or ill-treatment occurring in struggling families.

When we see documentaries about remote tribes whose ways of life have been relatively untouched by the industrial and post-industrial world, we see babies who can't yet walk, and sometimes even those who can, being carried in slings and wraps close to and touching whoever is carrying them. The most interesting thing about watching these documentaries is that you seldom hear a baby cry. This is not to say that we should keep our children close to us permanently. The steady increase of the time and distance between the child and the parent is important in his initial close connection and keeping them too close for too long can set them up for difficulties later in life too. It's about how one balances the time being close and being separate.

The pressures of day-to-day life these days often mean that parents are under financial pressure or the pressure of maintaining a career path to get back to work in a relatively short time after a new baby arrives. Knowing that this early connection is so important means that we can be conscious of focussing more on what is important when we are at home. Sadly though, many people also feel the pressure to maintain the image of a perfectly ordered house and active social life when a new baby arrives, which brings to mind a poem by Ruth Hulburt Hamilton that my aunt sent to me when my son was very small – sound advice I think

'The cleaning and scrubbing can wait till tomorrow

But children grow up as I've learned to my sorrow.
So quiet down cobwebs; Dust go to sleep!
I'm rocking my baby and babies don't keep'

Family Connections

When I talk about family and parents here, I am referring to the people who you were with when you were growing up – whether they were biologically related to you or not. What we need is the same, regardless of our social circumstances, and once we have passed through that early attachment stage, the next thing many of us have to deal with is siblings and the competing demands of other people in our family group.

Having a secure first connection with our parents is, unfortunately, not enough to maintain the feeling of safety and acceptance through the rest of our childhood, as other people come into the mix and we find that we are competing for the scarcest of resources – Attention

The attention of our parents is essential in keeping us safe and stable as we develop our identity. How we get that attention and what sort of attention it is also plays a big part in establishing our behaviour patterns and how we manage the relationships with others outside of our family. In a similar way to that first connection, not getting attention or recognition in our family is like not existing at all, and we will do whatever we need to do to get it. Positive attention is, of course, the best kind to get, and if that isn't available, we will get any kind of attention we can. Being shouted at is better than being ignored, and a slap is better than no physical contact at all. The bottom line is that people who seek attention do it quite simply because they need attention.

A few years ago, while on holiday, I saw a clear example of this playing out with a family by the pool. The family was made up of Mum and Dad and three children. James, who was about ten or eleven, a younger sister Amy, who looked about five, and a toddler called Oliver, who was obviously the baby of the family and so Mum and Dad were giving him a lot of attention. As the only girl, Amy also got a lot of attention, but James got very little and was expected to be quite self-sufficient and grown up.

To get attention, James would torment his sister, splash her, take her ball and throw it in the pool – just the general annoying big brother stuff. When this teasing created too many wails of protest from Amy, their father called James to him where he was sitting, and positioning James between his knees, he placed one hand on each of James' shoulders and spoke directly, firmly but calmly to him about his behaviour.

At that moment, James got the attention he needed with physical touch and eye-to-eye contact. He was, albeit briefly, the sole recipient of his dad's attention. It was negative attention, but that didn't matter; it was attention, and any attention is better than no attention at all. Then, the moment would pass, and the status quo resumed – Amy and Oliver would be praised and attended to, and James would be on the periphery until he began his attention-seeking behaviour all over again. And so, the pattern went on.

It isn't just the addition of new family members that can create this pattern if parents are not aware of how the older part of our brains translates the lack of attention as something that threatens our very existence – any competing interest can have the same effect. Work, television, social media – anything that takes a significant amount of the parent's attention away from the child, especially at times when the child is looking to interact with the parents, can set up this any-attention-will-do strategy.

Another example of this was a couple who brought their children for a meal at a local pub. The family were all very smartly dressed, and Mum and Dad sat next to each other with the children, a boy and a girl, sitting across the table. As soon as they sat down, the parents produced two tablets each with their own little headsets and placed one tablet in front of each child. The children sat there with their tablets propped up in front of them and their headsets on while Mum and Dad chatted with each other. Even when their food arrived, the tablets and headsets stayed in place. The little boy tried to speak to his parents a couple of times, and the response was to tell him to watch his video and to straighten the headset he was wearing back over his ears.

After a couple of attempts to interact with his parents, the boy started to get upset. He pushed his plate away, toppling the tablet and nearly knocking over his dad's glass. Both parents instantly paid attention to him until he settled down, and then the headset was back on, and they resumed their conversation. This happened another two times during their meal.

Another important thing about the attention we receive as children that influences our sense of identity and who we think we are is in our tendency to describe someone as being the behaviour that they are currently doing.

We very quickly generalise our experience of someone else's behaviour, and once we have experienced a similar behaviour a few times (and it does only take a few), our mind does what it does with all other experiences – it groups them together with other similar experiences and gives them a name, so we know how to recognise it. Knowing that this is a chair, this is a zebra and so on just saves time next time. We know what to expect and what to do the next time we encounter a similar thing. We do the same with people. 'You **are** a clever girl'. 'He **is** very rude'. 'She **is** very naughty' and so on. Notice that the person is being told that they are the behaviour and not just them actually exhibiting it. Not 'That was naughty', 'That was a rude thing to say' or 'That was a clever thing to do', but this is who you are.

It doesn't take many repetitions of a label before we start to comply with it and act it out as if it was true. At a time when our identity is being formed, being told who we are by a parent (or any authority figure) will form part of who we believe we are. We act accordingly and create evidence that aligns with their statements.

Our reality is constructed over time. We look for evidence that a belief is correct until it becomes real to us. We know it so well that we put it into our unconscious mind and let the programme run on autopilot. Here is an example of how easily it can happen:

A woman has two children a couple of years apart. The first child seems a little quiet, and the mother begins to think that maybe the child is shy or lacking in confidence, so she focusses on encouraging and coaxing the child to be more adventurous. When the second child arrives, the mother thinks that possibly this child is more confident and so she relaxes a little more around the second child in the belief that they will just progress nicely, propelled by the greater confidence that she thinks the second child has.

The first child notices that the mother is intervening in what they are doing to encourage them to do more and that the mother is not saying the same things to their sibling and so they interpret the coaxing as criticism. They begin to doubt their abilities and they start to lack confidence, confirming the mother's belief, and so she intervenes even more.

The second child sees the first child getting attention from the mother that they don't seem to get and tries harder and harder at whatever they do to get some of the attention. The mother sees the second child achieving and being proactive, and this confirms her belief that the second child is indeed confident and capable of getting on with things without intervention.

The mother's belief that she has a confident child and a child who lacks confidence is made real for all three of them. The first child feels criticised, the second child feels ignored, and both children believe that they are not good enough. It happens all very easily because of how our minds prefer to work. Although I doubt we can avoid generalising altogether, it's another area where being conscious of the labels we apply and the behaviours we engage in around other people is the first step to making better choices as we become aware of the potential impact our labels and behaviours may have.

There are 'good' girls and boys who have grown up being good and ultimately resenting the expectation but struggling to behave in any other way. There are 'bad' girls and boys who, as adults, will repeat 'I'm not really bad, you know' and struggle to stay out of trouble because that is how they got their attention. Many of us grow up feeling not good enough and not really knowing why. Sadly, we have, so far, not been great at unpicking and changing old beliefs and patterns of behaviour because of the 'Yes but….' response.

The 'Yes but…' response is what you quite often get from people when the subject of childhood experiences influencing adult behaviour and emotions comes up. It goes something like this:

'Yes, but…. that was a long time ago'.
'Yes, but…he/she is grown up now and should know better'.
'Yes, but…it wasn't that bad, get over it'.

It's the belief that the thinking of the top drawer and the in-tray are enough to sort anything out and all we need to do is apply a bit of logic, and the job's done. Sadly, it is not that easy. Rationalising by itself won't change anything, it will only, perhaps, explain it a bit better. We need to install a new pattern and new belief in the middle drawer to replace the old one, and while there are change techniques you can do with the help of a coach, there is a lot that you can start to build on for yourself too.

The Comparison Crisis

We naturally compare ourselves to the people around us. It's part of our tribal or pack nature and how we used to make sure we were part of the group. We would look around and check that we were sufficiently like the people around us and either modify something about our appearance or behaviour to make ourselves more like the group or run because this was not our pack and we were in big trouble!

This process has been going on for as long as we have lived in groups and we still do it, mainly unconsciously now. The way we dress, talk and move, what we believe is acceptable and what isn't will be within the accepted boundary of the group that we identify with. Even when teenagers rebel against the older generation and strive to be different, they generally do this by being the same as a different group from their family rather than just being different. It is all a part of our need to belong and knowing who we are. Even those who pride themselves on being different or unique will still make comparisons but adjust away from similarity, rather than towards it, because their identity is in being non-conformists.

Often, people resist the idea that they are making themselves like the group because we all like to think that we are individuals – and we are – and usually within a range of appearance and behaviour that is acceptable to our tribe, whatever that may be.

Outside of that range, we start to get very uncomfortable. A few years back, BBC2 ran a series called Tribal Wives, where women from the UK went to live for a month with a remote tribe and experience what it was like for women in that culture. One woman discovered that in the rules of the tribe she was living with, it was not acceptable for women to show their thighs but totally normal for them to go bare-breasted. She struggled with this because, to her, wearing shorts was perfectly normal but going topless was just not OK. So entrenched was the rule about not going topless that she found it impossible to fit in with the other women in this way.

As a species, we have evolved in a way that means we divide the human population into two distinct groups; there is 'Us', and there is 'Them'. Anyone who is one of Them is not of our tribe, not like us and even a lesser being than any of Us. Old tribal names demonstrate this well as many translate as The People, True People, Real People, People of this Land or Our People. Anyone outside of the tribe is then not true, real, our people or not of this land. The Us or Them part of our connection programme runs very quickly on encountering new people, and how we classify the new person, or people will determine how we behave towards them and respond to their behaviour. We will create a different meaning around any event involving one of Them than we would if it was one of Us. We will justify and make allowances for Us, and we will judge, accuse and ridicule Them.

You can see then how this becomes a problem for us when our tribal boundaries become blurred or expand into larger tribes with a looser definition. Our tribal boundaries are now more geographic than cultural or religious as used to be the case; so, how does our brain decide who is Us and who is Them? Complicate this again by belonging to more than one tribe, the geographic tribe and then one or more tribes within that tribe based on beliefs, preferences, interests or lifestyles. Add to this more complications with some of our tribes being virtual – existing only on social media and the internet. It is no wonder that people don't know whether they belong or are just fitting in.

It's not that we consciously want to divide the world into Us and Them; it is just that it is a comparison programme that the bottom drawer of our mind will run based on information from the middle drawer.

In theory, then, the whole process of comparison is to help us reconfirm that we are part of something, part of a group, belong to a tribe and know what the rules are. This sounds ok, and it was ok when our horizons were not as broad as they have become in recent years and the people we compared ourselves with were real, within reach and in the community that we belonged to. This is no longer always the case as the rise of the social media celebrity airbrushed images and rampant consumerism has left us comparing ourselves against ideals that are not only unattainable but, in many cases, just not physically possible. The advertising industry tells us that their product is just what we need to make us fitter/richer/slimmer/better-looking/cooler/more whatever it is we are told we need to be acceptable to the tribes we are trying to associate ourselves with. And we buy it.

It's not just that we are fed the message that we can do, have or be anything we want to. The message is that we *must* do, have and be *everything*, and if we are not constantly striving to be bigger, better and shinier in every aspect of our lives, then we are just not good enough, and we don't belong. We should, the message is, be setting ourselves goals to have more and more of everything.

It's great to have goals, to want to achieve or create something, to take pleasure and pride in working towards and reaching whatever the goal may be. When the goal is to have the latest and best of everything, the problem is that we never get to experience the joy and satisfaction of getting there because, as soon as we do, the goal moves on to the next thing that we seemingly can't live without.

We are endlessly dieting, covering our skin in chemicals, getting our faces numbed and pumped up because we don't look enough like an image that wasn't real in the first place. The endless churn of upgrades and the next 'must have' keeps many people in a constant state of 'not good enough' and our natural tendency to compare ourselves to others is leaving many of us feeling less like we belong and pushing us to try harder and harder to fit in. Less of an Us and more of a Them.

This crisis of comparison has contributed to the highest number of eating disorders, mental health issues and addictions so far in our history, as we have become the most obese, surgically-enhanced, and debt-burdened population to inhabit the planet to date. All this is because we fill the connection gap with whatever makes us feel better for a while.

This sounds a little depressing though, and it needn't be. We are doing a lot of this on autopilot, unconsciously buying into concepts without getting the full filing cabinet involved, letting the thinking of the middle and bottom drawer run our behaviour without getting the top drawer to think about it or even letting it into the conscious thinking that goes on in the in-tray.

To recover some of the lost connection that we so badly need, we need to get all three drawers of our mind involved in the process. First, to bring the importance of connection into our conscious awareness and then to use that awareness to build some new habits and new rules for living. Rationally redefining who Us is, means that we can consciously apply this when we meet new people, and by recognising when we have unconsciously classified someone as Them, we can overturn that decision and make Them part of Us. With sufficient repetition, our middle drawer will recognise the pattern and add this to the information it has stored for running this programme.

Another thing that we need for this, because reconnecting will take us outside of the place we are familiar with, is Courage.

Something to Practice - Reconnecting and Rewriting the Rules

Reconnecting with Others

Make eye contact – In our rushed lives, this is something that very often gets ignored as we are distracted much of the time. When you are at the checkout in the supermarket, when a colleague asks you something, when your kids talk to you or whenever anyone speaks to you, make eye contact with them. Remember, it's just eye contact – not a stare. There is a fine line between connecting and becoming too intense, especially when we are so unaccustomed to it.

Catch up in person – Arrange at least one face-to-face social meeting in a week (wherever possible). Coffee, lunch or anything that involves meeting one or more people face-to-face. Even if it's your partner or someone you regularly see in a work or family setting, arrange to meet in a different place and have a different conversation.

Say Yes – Say yes to an invitation that you would normally say no to and do your best to engage in whatever it is fully.

Reconnecting with Yourself

Give yourself a moment anywhere you can sit quietly for a while. Empty your in-tray (write down what you are thinking about and put it in your pocket for later if that helps) and breathe in slowly and deep down from and into your stomach. Imagine a warm light shining on the top of your head. Slowly allow that light to fill up your head and body from the top down, and as the light touches each part of your body, notice any pain or tension you are holding there and let it go. Notice any feelings or thoughts that are there and let the warm light wash over them right down to the tips of your toes. If you find yourself drifting onto other thoughts, say 'Just thinking' and return your focus to the light as it spreads through your body, increasing your relaxation.

There is an audio recording of a longer version of this meditation at https://www.being-human.today/resources that you can download and use as a guide if you wish.

Rewriting the rules

We learn a lot of rules when we are growing up about what we should and should not do. They are all of those things that you think to yourself that usually start with 'I must/mustn't', 'I should/shouldn't', 'I have to', 'I need to' or 'I don't/can't'.

Some of these are perfectly sensible and you would want to keep like 'Don't cross the road without checking for traffic' or 'Don't steal'. If you want the rule in your life, keep it.

Some of these are not quite so helpful and may prevent us from doing things that we want to. For example, one of my family rules was 'You don't blow your own trumpet', which made the idea of starting and promoting my own business something of a challenge and was a rule that I had to change.

You need three columns for this.

1. What are the rules that you are living your life by? What are the things that are 'just not done'?
2. Where did that rule come from? Whose voice do you hear when you think about the rule?

What would it have meant to have broken the rule? Why was it important to follow the rule?
3. What is the new rule that you are replacing it with? Make sure this is your rule for you. A good test for this is to ask yourself, "If I didn't follow this rule, what would it mean about me?". If the answer is that you are following the rule to make yourself more acceptable to other people, then this may not be one you want to adopt.

5 COURAGE

'You can choose courage, or you can choose comfort, but you cannot choose both' -Brene Brown

I have read a lot of self-help books and watched a lot of videos on the subject over the years. I have understood them, I have found them interesting and exciting (well, some of them anyway) and then I have walked away and carried on doing exactly what I was doing before. I didn't ignore them because I didn't want the benefits of the changes that the authors said I would get from following their suggestions or because I didn't believe they were possible. I stayed where I was because the vulnerability of change freaked me out, and I couldn't summon up the courage to move.

Courage isn't about being fearless. If you are fearless, you don't need courage, and I'm suggesting that we all have a little fear. Even people who generally care little for the opinion or approval of others will have something in their lives that makes them pause or put off doing something that they know is going to be uncomfortable for them. If you look up the root of the word 'courage', it comes from the word 'Cor', which means heart and courage originally meant to speak the truth from your heart. Over time, the use of the word has changed and is associated with bravado, acts of bravery and to keep going in the face of adversity, but it's the oldest meaning that this chapter focuses on. It's about being willing to step outside the boundary of who you think you must be and to be who you really are. To say it like it is for you and to put your ideas and creations out into the world. We all follow some rules about what's Okay and what's not Okay and what it means to be 'good' and 'responsible'. Making a change requires stepping outside of some or all of the rules and being seen for you.

You may have gathered now that this is probably the chapter where you decide if you are going to read the book and put it away or read the book and take some action around any or all of the six Cs in the book. As I said at the beginning, just reading a book is probably not going to get you much in the way of change. You will always need to take some action if you want to change anything about what you do and how you live your life, and the reason we are looking at courage at the same time as connection, creativity, compassion, consciousness and communication is that some of this might go against 'the rules' and I can pretty much guarantee that when you decide it's time to make some changes, not everyone is going to like what you are doing.

Although change is a big subject these days with thousands of books and courses created about how and what to change, your brain's processing system is not designed to like change; it is designed to recognise and like things that are the same. The equation we unconsciously work with is Same=Safe and Different=Danger because, when we were developing as a species, this was a life or death issue and anything that our brains identified as different needed to be treated as a potential threat. This basic process has not changed even though we have become more technically advanced. So strong is this equation of Same=Safe and Different=Danger that we will often stay in difficult and sometimes dangerous situations rather than move into the unknown. It is something that is called 'staying in your comfort zone' when, often, comfort has nothing to do with it. It's familiarity that keeps us there. People stay in jobs they hate and are bored by, in relationships that are over, even violent, and in lives that bring no joy or fulfilment because however uncomfortable a situation is, if it is familiar and we know how to act within it, it can feel less threatening than moving on to something new.

It is easy to underestimate how much we need familiarity to feel at ease. People around us recognise us by our appearance and our behaviour and recognise themselves in relation to us; therefore, change for us means change for them too. We can, to a point, cope with minor changes like a haircut or new clothes as long as they are not too far from the blueprint we have for that person in our mind. Once we start to make bigger changes, people start to become uncomfortable. And when the changes are about behaviour, beliefs and lifestyle, we can encounter some resistance or find that people struggle to accept the changes we are making. It doesn't matter how positive the change is or how much the ones closest to us agree that it is a good idea or say that they like change. If the change is significant, we can expect people around us to have some difficulty with it.

Family and friends are listed as number three of eight relapse triggers that can sabotage the efforts of a dependant drinker to stay sober, not because they don't care or want the other person to go on drinking but because their own behaviour is geared to knowing that person as a drinker, and they either haven't or are not yet prepared to change their behaviour to match a new way of relating to that person. This is how strong and how deeply unconscious the pull to stay the same and to maintain the status quo can be.

To think of it another way, if you can, imagine a child's mobile for a moment – one of those things that we hang from bedroom ceilings or over cots with different characters positioned along its arms. When all the characters stay in the same place, the mobile stays stable, and as soon as the position of any of the characters changes, the whole mobile is out of balance. There are only two ways to correct the imbalance: by putting the character back in its place or by adjusting all the other characters until a new balance is created. This is what the experience of change is like for us. When we see people changing around us, it is easier to push them back to their original position than it is to change ourselves to align with their new behaviour and beliefs. When we are changing, we have a choice whether to stay the same, because it is easier and more comfortable (even if we don't like it, familiarity is comfortable), to summon up the courage to start to change and then change back again because it's uncomfortable or to hold on to our courage, be who we are and wait until the mobile rearranges itself around us, which, I can tell you, it will. The characters will be in different positions or even be gone from the mobile altogether and be replaced by new characters, but a new stability will come.

With all this talk about the reaction of others to changes that we make, it could be easy to ignore the biggest threat to our ability to have and hold onto courage, because the person who is most likely to sabotage and stop our changes is, of course, ourselves.

Fear of Failure

For a long time now, we have had a strictly binary approach to failure and success. You either do one thing or the other, succeed or fail, and if you fail, your stop there. You're done. The reason most of us stop doing something is because we weren't good enough quickly enough to meet a predetermined interpretation of what 'good' or even 'good enough' looked like. If we don't go from beginner to expert really quickly, it is often enough to derail us.

Give this some thought for a little while: how many of us think that we can't do maths because we once got nervous when asked to answer an arithmetic question and the adult who had asked us the question became impatient? How many of us think we can never be good at sport because we came last in a race or didn't like PE at school? How many of us think we can't dance because we felt so clumsy that we never got as far as the dancefloor when everyone else looked like they knew what to do? How many of us have taken up a hobby, a musical instrument, a new sport only to drop it again because we were not good enough quickly enough and took it as failure?

Thankfully, not everyone buys into this, or we would be very short on technical developments and sporting achievements. Every new technical advancement comes to us on the back of multiple failed attempts. Edison is said to have made 1000 attempts to invent the light bulb, and when asked how he failed, is quoted as saying 'I didn't fail 1000 times; the lightbulb was invented in 1000 steps'. The difference between stopping and continuing is how we see the results of the efforts we have made. Instead of failure, Edison saw every unsuccessful attempt as something to learn from and build on. Athletes do the same; when they don't get the result that they were looking for, they analyse their performance to learn what they can do differently next time. If we really want to create change or create anything at all, this is the position we need to take. I'm not saying that there will be no feelings of disappointment or frustration when our efforts don't get us where we want to be as quickly as we would like, what matters is whether we respond to the disappointment by throwing in the towel or refocusing on what else we can do to get the results that we want. To put it simply:

There is no failure; there is only feedback.

When we look at a disappointing result as being a failure, we either stop altogether or throw out the work we have done so far and start again. Looking at the results as feedback means that we can not only think about what needs to change but also about what elements of what we did are good and worth keeping. I'm sure Edison didn't start back at the beginning again on every one of his 1000 attempts. It's true that the feedback might be that you would be better off following an entirely different path, and it is still only feedback. Failure has a finality about it. Feedback is about keeping your mind and your options open to learning and developing new ideas and projects. It's the difference between 'I didn't get it right' and 'I didn't get it right *yet*'. Adding the 'yet' keeps us in what is known as a Growth Mindset and helps us to stay resourceful and open to new ways of getting the results that we want. Taking and acting on feedback can only help us find better ways of working and get better results.

Don't fear failure, ask for feedback.

Who Do You Think You Are?

When we have called on our courage and got past our fear of failure, this the next thing that can stop us in our tracks: If you ask yourself 'Who do you think you are?' in your head without sounding even a little judgemental, I will be pleasantly surprised. It is one of the most commonly used phrases for putting someone 'back in their place' when they aim high or put themselves in the spotlight in some way. If we manage to get over the barriers of belief that we have to stay on our original career path, our habitual way of life and the belief set that we grew up with, quietening down the belief that we are not going to be good enough quickly enough, to do something new; when we get past all of that, this is what puts us back in our box.

We are taught that the way to succeed is to work hard, be good at the subjects that are chosen for you, follow the established progression as far as the education system says you are clever enough to go, apply to be accepted and wait to be chosen. We then apply to be accepted and wait to be chosen again and again as we climb the success ladder as far as we can, quietly, so as not to be seen as being a 'show off'. When the people higher up in the system decide that we have gone as far as we can go, we stay there, or at least we used to.

The way we work is clearly starting to change. There are more self-employed people in the UK every year as small independent companies come into being. Co-working spaces have begun to spring up in towns and cities, adding a new alternative to the traditional office and the potential isolation of working from home. People are stepping away from the familiarity of the corporate career ladder and finding new ways of working and doing business.

Breaking away and doing our own thing, whether in business or our lifestyles, means stepping forward and saying 'This is what I stand for, this is what I can do, this is what I can make and isn't it great?' It's probably time to take the tone of judgment away and ask ourselves who we think we are and then go out and be whatever that is.

Courage and Vulnerability

Stepping off the career ladder to start your own business creates vulnerability as you leave the safety of a regular income. Pitching a new idea to your leadership team creates vulnerability as you are open to rejection and the dismissal of your ideas. Exhibiting your first artwork to the public creates vulnerability as you wait to see what people make of your creation.

We have avoided the V word for a long time as our schooling and our commercial world has been run in an adversarial way. Whether we win or lose, or we succeed, or we fail, it's us versus them and we must show no weakness – showing vulnerability of any kind was lumped right in there as a weakness when it is very far from it. Being prepared to rework your invention 1000 times isn't weakness, standing up to speak to a room full of people when your knees are knocking isn't weakness, putting your work on display not knowing what the reaction is going to be is not weakness. Vulnerability is a position of strength because there is no longer any pretence to maintain.

Anything that involves doing something unfamiliar can be a vulnerable place to be, and it takes courage to be willing to be in that place. It can be very seductive to want to carry on playing it safe, and although things are undoubtedly changing, there are still more of us in the west who have been brought up with clear rules about what a 'proper job' is, why we have to have one and why we should wait our turn to be picked for the team by the next person up in the hierarchy. So, staying safe inside this model of the world is something that we know, as our unconscious processes will often choose the unsatisfying but familiar over the exciting and unknown.

To find the courage to do and be what we really want, we need to be able to get past the 'Not good Enough' feeling that most of us carry around in one or another of its three forms. Perfectionism is the form of 'not good enough', where we try to perfect everything – sometimes to the point of inactivity – because whatever it is hasn't been tweaked and perfected enough to show the world and we would rather not show up at all than show up looking less than perfect. Next on the list is 'just not good enough', where we are so not good enough that we won't even attempt something new. We decide that we are not going to be able to do it and would sooner not show up than risk being seen to fail. Finally, there is 'never good enough' (this was me by the way). This is where we turn up and put the effort in and even succeed. Having succeeded, we move the goal posts straight away and so wipe any notion of success, always being able to spot someone else who is better than we are.

To say 'I know this isn't perfect' or 'I know that I don't feel good enough and I'm doing it anyway' is courage and vulnerability in action together and the interesting thing with it is that it's contagious. The more we drop the act and say how it is, the more people around us do the same, and the perception that we have to be Teflon coated and flawless to get results begins to crumble; the more we start to build real connections.

The flip side of this though is that not all openness and sharing of experience means that we are allowing ourselves to be vulnerable. Sometimes early, oversharing of thoughts, beliefs and past experiences can be used as a defence mechanism or a shield. When we meet someone who tells us their life history or current personal issues up front before we get a chance to get to know them, it can often send us the message 'You can't criticise me because X happened to me in the past', 'I have a personal issue that means you have to go easy on me'. It keeps them safe, and it's not vulnerability, because the thing with vulnerability is that you're not safe, you're taking a risk. This also means that there is no requirement to be vulnerable in every situation or with everyone you meet. It's like any other risk we take in life, and it's a judgement call as to which risks we are going to take, what our purpose is in taking them and when. Let's face it, if it was really easy and we didn't believe that there was a risk, we would all just be doing it and no one would be squirming with 'not good enough' and wondering why it all seems so much easier when other people do it - because it's not, they are probably just better at bluffing.

A friend of mine, Nat, published her first book a few years ago and found herself thinking: 'What if nobody reads it…? Oh my god, what if somebody READS IT!!?' She had been writing for years but never made her work so public before, and at the last minute, the fear of her work being judged was far higher than of that of publishing and no one seeing it. She published it anyway. At the last count, Nat has published nine books. At the speed she writes, that will probably be ten or more soon, and she now approaches each new publication with excitement.

Like everything else in this book, having courage is a practice, and like many other things, it gets easier the more we do it.

Something to Practice – Celebrating Courage and Turning Failure into Feedback

Celebrating Courage

Sometimes we can be so busy being busy and getting on with things that we forget to notice how far we have come or what we have achieved. We put our time and energy into a project, complete it and move on to the next without pausing to appreciate the results of our efforts. We know that our mind needs to be told what we want it to focus on, so we need to train it to focus on how well we are doing rather than how much more we could have done.

The practice here is very straightforward: Plan it, do it, celebrate it.

We are already pretty good at the Plan it and Do it elements but tend to follow the Do it phase with Move on rather than acknowledging what we have achieved.

What you choose to do to Celebrate it can be as simple or as extravagant as you like. The important thing is what you are telling yourself about it and giving yourself some positive feedback. Sometimes, having a quiet moment of satisfaction is all we need. Sometimes, we need to party. It's your celebration; you choose what it needs to be.

Having a friend to share this kind of thing with is ideal. If you can share a celebration with another person, you get a real celebration synergy. Two people celebrating always feels like more than double the celebration that it would have been, had it been by yourself.

Failure into Feedback

When things don't go to plan, and your results are not what you want them to be, start getting into the habit of asking yourself 'What else can I do?', 'What can I do differently next time?' and 'What are the good parts of this that I want to keep the same?' If this is tricky at first because disappointment or frustration are getting the better of you, ask for feedback from someone that you trust. And remember, it's only feedback.

6 CREATIVITY

'Creativity is not the possession of some special talent, it's about the willingness to play'- John Cleese

The problem with creativity is that so few of us think we have any and fewer still would openly describe themselves as being creative.

I was discussing this recently with my friend Alison when I was talking to her about writing this book. "The thing is", I said, "that even though I know that creativity is such a vital part of being human and I'm writing a chapter saying that I believe that to be true, I don't feel like I am particularly creative myself." She just looked at me and laughed. "So, you're writing a book, you create training courses, you help people find ways to sort out their problems, and you can look at some random bits of food in your fridge and somehow turn them into a meal, but you're not creative? I see you as being very creative."

We chatted some more and realised that both of us saw the other as being creative but didn't connect with the idea of ourselves being creative people. Part of the reason for this, we believed, was in what we meant by 'creativity'.

To be creative, we realised, meant to be 'Good at Art'; and to be good at art, you had to have been told you are good at art quite early in life by your teachers and your family. Alison believes that she cannot draw and is, therefore, not good at art because once, aged about five, she had drawn a horse with a round head. She had been quite happy with her horse as she drew it but when she proudly showed her work to her teacher, she was left in no doubt that what she had done was wrong. From this she had concluded that she could not draw properly; therefore, she was no good at art. As we know, our RAS is very effective at going out and finding examples of what we believe to be true and then bringing us the evidence that we are right in our assumption; so, years later, despite some clear evidence to the contrary, she still believes that she is not creative.

When we get shamed as children for not being good enough, there is no wonder that we lose the desire and the willingness to try something creative when the price of being seen to fail is high. To be seen as not good enough is a form of rejection that can move us quickly from being one of Us to feeling like we are one of Them – an outsider. Not only do we then believe that we are no good at art, but we can also feel like we don't really belong to our tribe. It damages our self-worth and our sense of belonging. At its most basic level, rejection by the tribe threatens our very existence. Safer to stay below the radar than risk more rejection; safer to, perhaps, keep our ideas and creativity to ourselves and focus on fitting in. Sadly, this is how many of us live our lives.

We have made creativity competitive, and then valued competition above all else. We have made it about grades, attainment targets and standards. How you can have a creativity standard, I'm not entirely sure. Those two words just don't belong together; yet, so many of us will believe that we are not creative because somewhere along the line we didn't meet the standard expectation of us based on someone else's definition of what good looks like. We draw a horse that has a round head, we hit some flat notes in the school orchestra or write a poem that doesn't follow the structure being taught, and that's it – we're out of the entire creativity game. It's time to leave creativity to the talented kids. It's as if something only has value in it if other people think you are good at it and creativity for the pleasure of it has no worth. We seem to have forgotten that creativity is about experimenting, it is about having an idea and being open to seeing where it takes us, even if it takes us nowhere at all. It is, as the opening quote of this chapter so beautifully says, about the willingness to play. I wonder how many of us have had that willingness to play squeezed out by the pressure to be seen to be good at what we do, to pass tests, be serious and act like a grown up. How many of us see being a grown up as meaning we don't get to play anymore?

Not a proper job

Another problem with being tested on our creativity in the school system is how long we are allowed to keep experimenting with our abilities as we progress through school. If we make it over the 'no good at art' hurdle, the next obstacle between us and our creativity can be in how much it is or isn't valued by our families, school and peer groups.

Being creative, it seems, is OK for children or as a hobby, but not something to spend too much of your time on, and definitely not something you should allow to get in the way of academic success or the serious business of getting a 'proper job'. I overheard someone recently commenting to the woman next to her that it was great that the school's art and craft classes gave the less academic children something to do as if creative work is like therapy for the less academically inclined to keep them occupied while the bright kids get on with achieving. That's not education; that's training. It's as if we can be one thing or another, creative or academic, but like oil and water, they don't mix.

I was lucky and got to continue with Art to exam level at school. It was a fight to be allowed to do this, and I managed to get to keep art as a subject because I had a lot of academic exam subjects too. Therefore, it was decided that following this, one subject wouldn't be too much of a waste. It is true that I don't earn my living as an artist, but I also studied Chemistry, Physics and History, and I'm not a scientist or a historian either. So, should I see those subjects as a waste too?

We continue to insist on focusing our children's education only on the things that we believe can directly and positively influence their ability to get a 'good job' but not necessarily contribute to their development and well-being as an individual. It is not only creative subjects that this has happened to. Time and attention allowed for subjects like cookery (now called Food Technology, I understand) and other skills-based subjects have declined over time. I spoke to someone recently who told me that her son's Food Tech lesson had been to bring ready rolled pastry and a bag of grated cheese to school to make cheese pastries and that the marks were for presentation and appearance of the food not the ability to make it or any knowledge of the nutritional value. Sport has suffered a similar fate in many schools; combined with the prevalence of video games and social media, many of our children now spend less time outside than people who are in our prison system. I'm not saying that the more academic subjects are a bad thing, just that, again, it feels like we are out of balance and valuing only one aspect of our capabilities.

The paradox (or the hypocrisy, depending upon your viewpoint) is that when someone has held on to their creative interest and is seen to be talented, the same society that discourages creativity for its own sake as a waste of time and effort will hold these people in high esteem and even hero worships them. We have a fascination with film stars, famous rock bands and artists whose paintings sell for millions; we want to associate ourselves with them, to be like them and have what they have. They have made it to the top and that is something that is approved of, conveniently ignoring all the audition rejections, discarded paintings and unrecorded songs that have been part of the artist's journey to recognition. When there is enough money associated with it, something that wasn't a proper job becomes the envy of millions.

How many of us have been discouraged from seeing the creativity in what we do either by not valuing the creative process at all or by an insistence that we must be seen to be good at creativity to allow ourselves to engage in it? At what age do we stop praising every paint splodge created by a toddler and start picking fault with their ability to create accurate pictures of objects animals or landscapes? At what point in time did that become our definition of being creative?

I'm not suggesting that we should be praising every flick of a paintbrush or absent-minded doodle as a work of artistic genius. I'm suggesting that we need to separate achievement from creativity to see it for the vital part of our experience that it is and to recognise it wherever it may be found. We should be encouraged by, and encouraging of experimentation for its own sake and of engaging in something that interests and excites us without any expectation of what it may become. It seems though, that in the western world, we have attempted to separate creative thinking from logical thinking as if they were not connected to each other in any way, when we really need both. Look at anything that we would recognise as a great achievement in medicine, science, architecture or engineering; none of them would have made it into existence without the ability to be both creative and logical in our thought processes.

By making creativity and art synonymous and then making art a pass or fail situation, we are restricting our view of and access to our basic creativity as human beings.

Anything new, any changes to something that already exists, any new use for something that we already have, any change of any kind has a creative element to it. So, maybe what we need is to find the creativity in what we already do and value it for what it is, because whatever we do for a living or as a hobby, any activity that gets us into that state of mind where we can lose ourselves in what we do is as good for us and our wellbeing as any form of meditation.

It has been known for a long time that engaging in any creative process is good for our mental and emotional health. Self-expression can help us deal with difficult feelings, find solutions to problems and increase our sense of connection. Having a creative outlet can lower our stress levels and our blood pressure, and therefore, contribute to our physical as well as our mental health and wellbeing. Art therapy has been part of the process in the healing professions for many years. So, if creativity is good for healing, maybe we could be doing more of it now, while we are well? They say that prevention is better than cure and maybe we need to see it as something that is for everyone and not just for small children, recovering patients and the talented few.

The Fear of Being Seen

While we move towards exploring our creativity, there is something else that can stand between us and our natural creative selves. It's a fear that feels similar to the fear of failure and is almost the exact opposite of it. It's the fear of being seen.

When we have grown up with a sense of not feeling good enough (most of us have), being seen can be as hard to handle as being ignored.

When I talk about being seen, I am not referring to the way that you see someone in the street or at the office. I mean really be seen for who we are, our ideas, hopes, dreams, fears and passions. The fear of being seen, or more accurately the fear of the response that we might get when we are seen, can be excruciating and is one of the many reasons why, for example, speaking in public has been quoted as being the most common fear in the US. Fear of dying is second on that list, so yes, some people apparently, would rather die than stand up and be seen.

You will know if you are struggling with a fear of being seen because when you are getting ready to deliver a presentation, show someone something that you have made, propose some changes at work or voice an opinion that you think might not be widely accepted, all you will see in your mind is the people you think are most likely not to like it and you start running the 'what if' script. 'What if they don't like it?', 'What if they say its rubbish?', 'What if they think I'm stupid?', 'What if they think I'm arrogant?', 'What if?', 'What if?'. You'll notice that none of the what ifs are saying 'What if they love it?', or '"What if think it's a great idea?' It's a fear that we learn early in life – a fear of being seen as unacceptable and rejected by our tribe. It's different from the fear of failure because the fear of failure is about being seen to do something to an unacceptable level and fear of being seen is a fear of being unacceptable. It's the thing that pushes a lot of us to keep trying to fit in, to avoid standing out and that can stop us from bringing more creativity back into our world long after the requirement to be good at it in school has passed.

When we start to create something, anything at all, we are putting a little bit of ourselves out into the world. We often need courage to help us along, which can feel like a vulnerable place to be, and it is, because we are taking a risk. It's a risk that things may or may not work out as we hoped, that some people may not like what we have created. If we have taken a risk before and it hasn't worked out, we can be reluctant to take the risk and to feel vulnerable again, but the risk doesn't mean that something bad is going to happen. Risk is just a state of uncertainty, and the outcome of taking a risk can also be something hugely rewarding. Vulnerability is the feeling of sitting with that uncertainty, and just as it is with change, without a little vulnerability, there is no creativity.

I love the work of Brene Brown, whose writing I have quoted at the start of the last chapter. She has a fabulous way of describing what sometimes happens when we jump in with both feet and do something that is a long way from our normal behaviour patterns. It's the 'Vulnerability Hangover', and it goes something like this. 'Oh my god, what did I do that for? What on earth possessed me? What made me think that this would be a good idea?' It can feel like the world is about to end, because when we have been focused on fitting in for a long time, and then allow ourselves to be seen for who we are, the risk of rejection can seem huge.

I am not a social media expert. I post occasionally, and I'm not as at ease with it as many others are. I have never liked having my photo taken and seldom share pictures that have me in them, so making a video and posting it on Facebook was a bit of a stretch to say the least. I had signed up to do a run for cancer research and thought that uploading a few short videos might help to get some sponsorship. I thought that maybe one a week on the countdown to the run about a different aspect of coaching might be a good idea. I set off with Alison (who I'm sure was grateful that we weren't going to be drawing any horses) to the park where the race would eventually be held and where we made my first video on my phone.

I decided to post it a day or so later and was in a hotel room close to where I was working when I posted it. Sitting on the bed in my room, I faffed about for a long time avoiding the moment where I would click on the Post icon. Eventually, I clicked on Post. It was done. I panicked and called Alison. How she knew what I was saying is a mystery since my voice was so high pitched you would think only dogs could've heard it, as I ran the whole catastrophe prediction at top speed. Why had I thought that would be a good idea? What an idiot and what a crap video to post too! Stupid! Stupid! Stupid! She listened patiently to my high-speed drama, and eventually, I found my way back to earth and we laughed about it. Oh well, it was done now.

No catastrophe occurred, and in the morning, I was pleasantly surprised to find that the world had not ended. Some people posted supportive comments for what I was doing, some gave it a like or a share, and I got some money in my fundraising page. That was all. The only person judging what I had done in any negative way was me. When I stopped posting the videos on completing the run, a few people even asked if I was going to do some more.

If you have had a similar school experience regarding Art like the one Alison had, or if you have long since left any creative things that you used to do behind, and you want to start being more creative again, don't be surprised if you find yourself with the occasional vulnerability hangover. Know that it's better to feel a little vulnerable than to play it safe and leave your creativity gathering dust.

This is where the contents of this chapter link with the previous chapter and with the next one. We need to call up some courage to say 'I'm doing this' and then to do it. Courage is what gets us past the fear of being seen. Compassion (and, ideally, a friend with a good sense of humour) is what gets us past the vulnerability hangover.

Something to Practice – The Art of Being You

It is more difficult to suggest something specific to practice because how I define creativity will differ from how you define it. What might be ideal for me might just not inspire you at all. Therefore, this is more a case of giving you some things to consider and decide what you want to practice.

The one thing I am going to suggest that you practice is making whatever form of creativity you decide to play with a part of your life. You may need to make a date with yourself at first, until it becomes a part of your life, but playtime is important, however old we think we are.

If you have a friend or family member to go and do some of this with, that's great. Remember to focus on your interpretation of what creativity is to you.

If you give the following questions a little thought, the answers will help to lead you in the creative direction that is right for you.

What are the things that you currently do that have a creative element to them?

What do you do to relax?

Did you have a hobby when you were younger that you used to enjoy and no longer do?

Would you like to do it again?

What thoughts, beliefs or fears have stopped you?

Are any of these reasons Clutter and Nonsense? (See Chapter 2)

How many of them can you remove from the list?

Is there anything you have always wanted to try that you haven't?

What thoughts, beliefs or fears have stopped you?

Are any of these reasons Clutter and Nonsense? (See Chapter 2)

How many of them can you remove from the list?

Is there anything that you do now that you would like to do more of?

What thoughts, beliefs or fears have stopped you?

Are any of these reasons Clutter and Nonsense? (See Chapter 2)

How many of them can you remove from the list?

Pick something from the list of things you want to do, and go out to play.

7 COMPASSION

'The compassionate mind is the mind that transforms'
– Paul Gilbert

Of everything that I have read and studied in the last ten years, this is probably the one from the six Cs in this book that has been hardest to wrap my head around, especially where self-compassion is concerned.

The rule book, as it was in my mind back then, was very clear. You get on with it. No taking time off unless you cannot physically get up and out of the door. Go in to work early, leave late, take work home and never ignore a call or an email. Struggling to cope was a sign of weakness, and self-care was just a cop out and an excuse not to pull your weight. I was as resentful of people who cut themselves some slack as I was incapable of cutting some slack for myself. So, you can imagine my reaction then when I realised that I should pay attention to self-compassion. 'We need to what? Really? Oh, for goodness sake!!' (or words to that effect, I'm sure you get the picture). The rule has been that you love other people – not yourself. That's something that only arrogant or very selfish people do, and I wouldn't want to be seen as being one of those people, now would I? Little did I realise then that rather than being an indulgence that would stand in the way of success, compassion is essential if we want to experience success with our mental, physical and emotional health intact. Because here's the thing; we are all doing the best we can with what we have. It's as simple as that. Maybe not the best we could ever do in perfect circumstances, not the best ever or a record-setting best but our best right now at this moment.

Simple as that statement is, it took a while to sink in. The phrase 'doing your best' had always been closely associated with being a high achiever and doing your absolute best, winning and striving to be 'the best' in comparison against the best that others were achieving. Letting go of comparing myself to other people, of a need to be the best rather than being my best is a necessary, sometimes tricky step on the way to a more compassionate mind because compassion is at the core of what makes a human being a humane being.

Compassion is an awareness of the suffering or struggle of others and of ourselves, and a desire and a will to relieve it. It underpins our connections and our sense of belonging and is fundamental to our wellbeing and happiness. We, I'm sure, are all too aware of the acts of anger and hatred that human beings are capable of. It's compassion that can begin to heal the scars of disconnection and separateness and move us away from an Us and Them mentality, and towards being all of us in this together. It is a vital, primary human emotion and yet, particularly over the last 50 years, we have marginalised it in favour of competition, material wealth and getting ahead.

There was, for a while, a more community-centred way of thinking with the creation of the welfare state and National Health Service in the UK during the post-war years of the forties and fifties. Sadly, this did not last, and we have moved increasingly away from a community focus and towards a system which, while making us (or at least some of us) financially better off, undermines some of our basic needs as human beings.

Since the 1970s, the way we work, do business and educate our children has had a profound impact on the expectations we have of ourselves and everyone else around us. We have been educated and trained to take our place in a business structure where the creation of wealth for the shareholder through ever increasing earnings and growth has been the prime concern of corporations and the absolute measure of what success means. The concepts of self-reliance and personal responsibility have morphed into a growing sense of entitlement and attitude of 'Me first' and of rights without responsibility. We have been so intent in the pursuit of getting more and more from less and less that we run the risk of being dehumanised by it.

I have worked with UK companies where no one wants to be seen to be the first to leave when the time to go home arrives and seemingly endless rounds of redundancies and restructures keep the workforce in a permanent state of confusion and uncertainty. I have worked with US-based businesses where 'at will' contracts, where employment can be terminated at any time, hang over the heads of employees as they give up their evenings, weekends and their already brief holidays to hit increasingly demanding targets to counter the endless mood swings of the stock market.

We habitually spend more time working than we are paid for, we skip our breaks and eat 'al desko' and buy the myth that multitasking is something that we can and should be doing rather than something that, in reality, creates more stress and results in poor performance when we attempt it.

I'm not arguing that we should abandon

efficiency and focus entirely on the needs of the community because I don't think that it is an 'either-or' situation. It is, as most things are, about balance and it's that balance between success as wealth creation and success as wellbeing creation that needs addressing.

It starts with you

We are harder on ourselves than we are on anyone else and would probably not accept other people talking to us in the way that we talk to ourselves. If we pay attention to what we are saying to ourselves in our thoughts, it probably won't be long until we call ourselves 'stupid' or 'idiot' (or worse) and remind ourselves that we think we are not good enough in some way or another. The way that we talk to children becomes their inner voice when they become adults so the words we use to beat ourselves up with will be words that we had heard at home or in school when we were growing up. It doesn't mean that people around us were particularly or deliberately nasty to us. They were, as we have seen, just repeating the language and behaviour patterns that they learned from their parents, who learned the same from their parents and so on right back as far as you care to go. Here's an example of how easily our experiences become part of that inner critical voice:

When I was very small, about three years old, I was at my Nana's house with my sister. I was in the living room, and my sister and my Nana were in the kitchen. There was an open fire in the room, and a spark jumped from the fire and onto the cushion of the chair beside it. The cushion immediately began to smoulder, and I ran into the kitchen. "Nana, the chair is smoking!" I said. She, being busy and a little annoyed at the interruption, replied "Don't be stupid", but I insisted, and she grudgingly investigated. Her mood did not improve when she found out that the chair was indeed smoking, and she dealt briskly with the smouldering ember before going back to whatever it was she was doing in the kitchen without further comment to me.

At the time of writing, this memory is fifty years old and is, of course just my recollection of what happened and not necessarily the full picture. For it to be such a clear memory though would suggest that, however inaccurately I may or may not be recalling it, it was significant to me at the time. Small wonder then that my go-to inner critic phrase is 'Don't be stupid'. It doesn't mean that I am traumatised or badly done to, it's just an example of how quickly we take meaning from a situation, act it out and play it back as if it were true and ignoring any evidence to the contrary.

This is why, when it comes to working with compassion and compassionately leading our lives, it all has to start with us. If we set out trying to be compassionate to everyone else but not to ourselves, we will start to prioritise other people's wants and needs ahead of our own all the time (if we were not doing that already). We will make allowances for situations and behaviours that are not acceptable to us and all our boundaries will become blurred. When we attempt to practice one-way compassion, what we end up with is not a feeling of compassion for others, it is resentment. Then, we will beat ourselves up again for feeling resentful when we are supposed to be being compassionate, and so it goes on.

We have all been criticised at some time in our lives. We have all done things that we are not necessarily proud of and maybe wish we hadn't done, and unless we are psychopathic, we all feel a little shame from time to time. These are all normal events in the human experience, and not, in themselves a problem. The problem is in the story we tell ourselves about them and the language we use when we do. The only person who can let us off this particular hook is ourselves.

In a similar way to what happens when we try to be compassionate to others but not to ourselves, one-way compassion doesn't work when it is just coming from other people to us but not from us to ourselves. When we lack self-compassion and are faced with someone else's attempt to show compassion to us, we may feel like they are patronising us or it might bring up more shame as we tell ourselves that we shouldn't need someone else's sympathy because we should be stronger/working harder/more resilient and so on.

When you start to practice self-compassion, you will probably need to use a little courage too. Courage is necessary because of the response of others when you start saying no when you used to say yes and want to change old routines to ones that are better for you and also because of what you are likely to be saying to yourself. When we have been telling ourselves to get on with it and reminding ourselves that we think we are idiots and stupid, it can take a while to quieten the internal monologue down; therefore, keep in mind that it is a practice for progress and not for perfection. However tempting it may be, please don't add it to the list of things to beat yourself up about. I'm still working on this. Am I thinking all the time compassionately? No. Do I get judgmental sometimes? Oh yes! Indeed, I do, and I'm just doing the best I can with what I have; it's a work in progress.

Not all bubble bath and chocolate cake

Self-compassion means not beating ourselves up for not being a superhero all the time or for things in the past that we can't go back in time and fix. It's about giving ourselves a break without getting to the point of withdrawing from the world in a way that makes it more difficult to do things differently in the future. There can be a temptation, when we start to think about self-compassion or self-care, to translate the meaning of self-care into being exclusively about cancelling appointments, saying 'no' to requests for our time and having a lie in, a long bath or a cream cake. While self-care may indeed include some or all of these things, it's not all that it is.

If we are running ourselves into the ground with a gruelling schedule of tasks and demands on our time, then we do probably need to find ways to lighten the load and relax so that we can catch our breath. We may also need to consider some other aspects of self-care too, if we want to avoid getting into a cycle where we have periods of over-committing and generally overdoing anything followed by a period of having to withdraw and get back into the bubble bath.

Self-care is as much about getting us back up off the sofa and putting the wine glass down as it is about getting us to sit on the sofa in the first place. It's about focusing on what is best for us – whether that's taking ourselves off the treadmill for a while or getting ourselves up and moving in a way that is going to drain us less than it was before. It's almost like being our own parent and giving ourselves some new more empowering rules to live by than the ones we have adopted along the way. If you were dealing with an upset child or teenager, part of the solution might be a treat of some kind and rest, and I am pretty sure you would also be advising them and suggesting new and better ways of doing things to help them in the future. This is no different than what we need to do for ourselves.

When we practice self-care and self-compassion, its best to do it consciously and not assume that what someone else does or recommends for their own self-care will serve the same purpose for us. Ask yourself what care and support are needed. What are you planning to do to get that need met and how will this serve that purpose and help you to move forward? It's absolutely fine to go to your favourite comfort blanket, be it chocolate, wine or literally your favourite blanket. Be conscious that this is what it is, and while it will soothe your feelings at the moment, you may need to follow that up with something else to get you on the path that you really want to be on. Getting 'back on track' is not the aim of self-care. If you are not on a track you want to be on, all the duvet days in the world are not going to change that or ultimately give you the right level of self-care and compassion for what you really need.

Beware the Positivity Police

It is well-known now that we operate better in a positive mindset than we do in a negative or stressed state. Our performance is better, our health is better, and the outcome we get from our actions is more positive too. Insisting that everyone comes from a positive mindset all the time, however, is not the best way to encourage positive thinking. Sadly though, a requirement to be positive can be, and often is, used to shut people up or to keep them in line. Relentless, insistent positivity can be as draining and stifle creativity just as much as persistent negativity – it's all about balance and perspective.

We are not by nature designed to be consistently positive, and it is part of our default settings to be on the lookout for risk. It is one of the reasons that we have survived and thrived as a species so well for so long. If we had skipped out of the cave each morning without taking the time to scan the area for potential threats, then we would have been more likely to end up being lunch than to live long enough to eat lunch. Looking for potential threats and thinking about what could go wrong with a view to taking some action to avoid them is not only not negative, it's a sensible, positive thing to do if we want to move forward with whatever it is we are doing. It's true that worrying about every possible issue that could arise and not taking action is not going to get us very far, and neither is mindless, unquestioning positivity. We are not going to get the results we want without taking action of some kind towards where we want to get to. What we do with the thoughts that we have, be they positive or negative, makes the difference in our direction of travel. Whether the thoughts we have are generally positive or negative helps to determine the experience we are having in the now, and we need a balance of both. We need enough positivity to keep us in a growth mindset and enough negativity to sense check our plans.

We can sometimes be guilty of rushing people who have just experienced a difficult situation or event to see the positive that can be found in it. This, I believe, can be as unhelpful and unhealthy as leaving someone stuck in negativity indefinitely. It is undoubtedly inspirational to hear the stories of people who have suffered a loss or faced illness or injury and used what they have learned from it to build something new to help themselves and others. We just need to allow people the time and space to get there and not push positivity at them too soon. We need to let them process big life-changing events. It seems that, in the name of positive thinking, we have just changed our method of emotional repression while still doing everything we can to avoid having to deal with any kind of upheaval in ourselves or in others. We used to expect people to be back at their desk and 'back to normal' the day after the funeral of a close friend or relative, or as soon as the doctor says they can come back after a major injury or illness. Now, it seems that 'back to normal' isn't enough and the new expectation is that they have 'found the positive' in whatever has happened and are already a better, stronger and more resourceful person for the experience that they have only just had.

The difficulty with this can be in knowing how long is long enough. How long does grief last? How long do we need to recover from a life-changing event? It's difficult to say. What I will say is that if someone suffers a major loss one day and has discovered their life's new purpose the next, it is probably too soon and more to do with avoiding the pain than learning and growing from adversity. We need to be patient and compassionate. It's their experience and their choice in what, when and if they learn from it. Not ours.

Something to Practice: Clearing the SMOG for a new perspective

SMOG Detection

SMOG is all about the Shoulds, Musts, Oughts and Got Tos that we use to get ourselves running around doing stuff that we think we have an obligation to do or because we think we will be seen as selfish or cold-hearted in some way if we don't. Running our lives on a list of SMOG obligations generates resentment and gets in the way of compassion.

Start to look out for SMOG in your thoughts when you are talking and then consider the following: Who says you Should/Must/Ought/Got To?

What will happen if you don't?
What will happen if you do?
What won't happen if you do?
What won't happen if you don't?
What is the reason or purpose for doing it?
How do you feel about doing it? Who does it help?
If you didn't feel that you Should/Must/Ought/Got to, would you still want to do this?
What could you/might you do instead?

A new perspective - If I were you…

We are often pretty good at giving helpful advice to other people, and this practice is about beginning to do that for ourselves.

When you are feeling overwhelmed or have just made a mistake (or any situation where you are not feeling great about yourself), find yourself a quiet moment and follow this process.

Ask yourself the following questions in the context of this problem:

What do you see?
What do you hear?
What do you think?
What do you feel?

Then, take up the view point of someone else who knows you and can see what's going on. To the best of your ability, try to be that person and ask yourself again:

What do you see?
What do you hear?
What do you think?
What do you feel?

Then, take up the viewpoint of a complete outsider to this who does not know you at all but can see what's going on. To the best of your ability, try to be that person and ask yourself:

What do you see?
What do you hear?
What do you think?
What do you feel?
What advice would you give to this person that would help them with this problem?

Finally, back from your own perspective, how would it be to take on the piece of advice that you have just received?

It can be useful to physically change the position you are sitting and standing in between each stage of this process to reinforce to your mind that you are looking at this from a different perspective.

There is a video demonstration of this at https://www.being-human.today/resources.

8 TIME TO REBOOT

'There is nothing either good or bad but thinking makes it so' – William Shakespeare

Before 2007, when I began to look at why we believe what we believe and do what we do, I thought that my experience of the world came from the outside. I believed that the events that I experienced, and the actions of other people were responsible for whether I was happy or unhappy and whether things worked out for me or not. Reality was objective, and I was just reacting to it. Thankfully, I no longer live in that world or believe that to be the case.

When we look at a rainbow, we don't see its colours as they are, because there are so many aspects of light and colour that our brains can't process. We don't see it as it is, we see it according to how we are and what we process in our mind. My current understanding is that our whole experience of life is like this and we don't so much experience the world as it is. We experience it as we are. I didn't experience my job in finance; I experienced my thinking about my job in finance. I don't experience my life with my family; I experience my thinking about my life with my family. This sounds all very simple, and it is; what complicated it for me was about fifty years of not realizing that and taking my interpretation of experiences and what I thought about them to be a solid and unchangeable reality.

We have our experiences in one long continuous 'now'. Wherever we are, and whatever we do, it is always now. We get all tangled up though because a lot of our thinking is about our interpretation of things from the past that are no longer happening, and our imagination about things from the future that haven't yet happened. We hold on to our negative feelings from past events and worry about our plans for the future not working out as we would like. The more we do it, the more we think it's all real, because the RAS and the filing cabinet will follow our instructions and seek out evidence that it is all true. When we have enough evidence for a long enough period, we not only believe that it is true, we can also come to believe that it is permanent.

How many times have you heard someone say 'I'm too old to change now' or 'You can't teach an old dog new tricks'? We often think that our ability to change our thinking and behaviour is somehow linked to the amount of time that we have held a belief or acted in a certain way. It's as if the time we have been thinking or doing something should be equivalent to the time it will take you to change it, that the effort required to change should be equivalent to the impact our old thinking has had on our lives, and that, somehow we devalue our problems or dishonour our memories if we let go of them too quickly and easily.

I once heard this analogy that I think is a great way of explaining where we can sometimes find ourselves. I can't remember where I heard it, but I do think it's useful here.

When we are born, we are like diamonds – bright, shiny and beautiful and full of potential. As we go through life, we encounter the bullshit of other people's thinking, and because we look to these people for guidance, we allow some of the bullshit to stick. Soon, we realise that we are covered in bullshit and don't like it, so we generate some different bullshit of our own and cover up the stuff other people gave us. Eventually, the bullshit layer is so deep that we forget about the diamond and think that we are bullshit to the core. We don't like how we feel about that, so we roll ourselves in glitter to cover it up, panicking whenever a little bullshit shows through the shiny coating and forgetting completely the beauty that lies at the centre.

When we recognise the bullshit for what it is, we can quite quickly get back to the things that really matter because we are not a product of our past, although we often think that we are. We are the product of what we think about our past.

Even if we are thinking about an event from the past or imagining an event from our future, we are doing that now, and if that thinking is causing us a problem, that is also happening now. So, we can change that now too. Our thinking is everything, and at the same time, it is just thinking; the beauty of that is that we can change our thinking and change our minds whenever we choose. We can rewrite whatever we bring up from the filing cabinet and into the in-tray in a way that works better for us before we file it away again.

In the same way that we can reboot a computer programme that is not functioning as it should, we can do the same for our thinking, and in turn, our experience of life, resourcefulness and wellbeing. When we find that our thinking has been keeping us overwhelmed with the anxiety of too much clutter and nonsense, and that we are held back by beliefs that we can't even consciously remember creating, we can reset the programme and reboot our life experience. What many of us have been doing so far is adding on new programmes, new apps and more gadgets to the system in the hope that these add-ons will make us achieve more, have more and be more. Instead, what we need to do is get under the bullshit and back to the foundation that all the rest of our thinking is sitting on.

We are, at our core, conscious beings capable of insightful communication and deep connection. We are creative, courageous and compassionate by nature, and despite all the political, financial and technological upheaval that goes on around us, when we clear out the nonsense and clutter from the in-tray, I believe that these six Cs of our operating system are what being human is really all about.

ABOUT THE AUTHOR

A ten-year journey of reading, discovering and stepping far outside the familiarity zone has taken Anne Burton from the world of finance and spreadsheets to training, coaching and writing on all aspects of who we are and why we do what we do. She believes that we massively underestimate our ability to change unhelpful habits, beliefs and behaviours and to get back to being the amazing beings that we are. Anne lives in Derbyshire with her husband John and dog Frank. She loves holidays with the family and a gin and tonic (sometimes together and not necessarily in that order) and hates having to write about herself in the third person.

CPSIA information can be obtained
at www.ICGtesting.com
Printed in the USA
LVHW08s1611240918
591186LV00035B/985/P

9 781533 606815